UNWRAPPING the SERVANT

TEACHING KIDS to SERVE JESUS and OTHERS

Tina Houser

Warner Press, Inc
Warner Press and "WP" logo are trademarks of Warner Press, Inc

Unwrapping the Servant: Teaching Kids to Serve Jesus and Others
Written by Tina Houser

Warner Press Kids™, an imprint of Warner Press, publishes ministry resources designed
to help children grow more deeply in their faith.

Scripture quotations used in this book were taken from the following:

ESV–*ESV® Bible (The Holy Bible, English Standard Version®)*, copyright © 2001 by Crossway Bibles,
a publishing ministry of Good News Publishers. Used by permission. All rights reserved.

(NASB)–*New American Standard Bible®*. Copyright © 1960, 1962, 1963, 1968, 1971, 1972, 1973, 1975, 1977, 1995
by The Lockman Foundation. Used by permission. (www.Lockman.org)

(NIV)–*HOLY BIBLE, NEW INTERNATIONAL VERSION ®. NIV®*. Copyright © 1973, 1978, 1984, 2011 by Biblica, Inc.®.
Used by permission. All rights reserved worldwide.

(NLT)– *Holy Bible, New Living Translation* copyright© 1996, 2004, 2007 by Tyndale House Foundation.
Used by permission of Tyndale House Publishers Inc., Carol Stream, Illinois 60188. All rights reserved.

Requests for information should be sent to:
Warner Press Inc
1201 East Fifth Street
P.O. Box 2499
Anderson, IN 46012
www.warnerpress.org

Editors: Robin Fogle and Karen Rhodes
Cover & Interior Designer: Christian Elden

ISBN: 978-1-59317-781-2

Printed in USA

TABLE *of* CONTENTS

TABLE *of* CONTENTS

INTRODUCTION

Dear Servant of God,

It has been the desire of my heart to write this book for a long time—ever since I took the first group of 9 second-graders through an intensive 6-week program focused entirely on what it means to be God's servant and on putting that into action. Now those kids are entering college, and some of them are going into ministry. All of them, though, were different after that particular 6 weeks. The effects of those servanthood experiences didn't wear off in a week or two but changed their lives and greatly impacted their spiritual foundation. Their serving potential had been *unwrapped*.

I've also seen how serving together as a family affects kids. In fact, Willow Creek Association conducted a study where they surveyed 1,000 churches and 250,000 believers that revealed the "most catalytic action"—the most effective method—for making disciples is to serve together, not by yourself (Willow Creek Association/MOVE). Servanthood is a shared experience where people grow spiritually. A critical foundation stone of a child's spiritual development is learning to serve, especially alongside a parent.

This book is not intended for children's ministry workers alone, but for parents, families, grandparents, and anyone who has influence over a child. All of these activities are "good" things to be involved in, but central to our serving is our gratitude for what God has done for us, and our obedience to Him. In His Word He tells us that our lives will be complete when we love one another and express that love through serving. We cannot neglect this holy habit.

As you flip through these pages, you will feel comfortable with some of the activities and projects, and others you won't. Some will fit your facilities, resources, and the skills of your kids, and others will not work in your situation. Some may be something you want to undertake, and others won't resonate with you. Some even may feel a little unsafe to you. As you read, I pray you will be challenged to figure out how these projects can be creatively tweaked so your kids will get the greatest benefit from them. However you choose to get your kids involved, just do it!

Zechariah 4:10 tells us that the Lord rejoices when we begin. He rejoices when our empathy and sympathy become compassion, leading us to respond to the needs of others. Stop talking about it and nodding your head that it's a good idea, and start changing the mindset... the heart throb...the worldview...of the kids you have influence over. Lay the foundation for a servant's heart that will become a cornerstone of their faith development. Unwrap the servant God has within each child. It's a beautiful present to unwrap!

Counting it a joy to serve our incredible God alongside you!

tina!

UNWRAPPING COMPASSION

Compassion is sympathy ("Sorry this happened to you and that you're going through this") and empathy (being sensitive to the feelings of others) blended together, with action thrown in.

Compassion is

recognizing a need ...

being touched by it ...

and taking a step to help.

Don't Wait! Since the brain is developing faster in the three-year period between 3-5 years of age, we need to be teaching about compassion at this young age, rather than waiting until kids get older.

Once kids grasp what compassion means and they have regular opportunities to exercise it, compassion becomes the foundation for the "normal" and the "right" thing to do.

We love one another because Christ first loved us!

Consider the following points to help you unwrap the compassion God has placed in your child(ren). These are basic concepts you may assume everyone understands ... but they don't. They are basic teaching methods you may assume everyone uses ... but they don't. They are basic considerations that need to be ingrained in our attitudes to help us become sensitive to numerous needs ... maybe going unnoticed in our own backyard.

Do a self-evaluation.

Conduct this self-evaluation with the kids. They should answer "yes" or "no" to each of the questions by using these gestures: open palms facing up mean YES and palms facing down mean NO. You could also use black and white gloves or smile and frown plates.

- Do you enjoy giving something away?

- Are you good at listening when people tell you how they feel?

- Are you kind to other kids, adults, and people you don't know?

- Are you ever mean?

- Do you demand your way without thinking of others?

- Would you ever give up doing something you want to do to help someone else?

The answers to these questions will give the kids an idea of what they personally understand and the leader a feel for what a "win" looks like as they prepare to help kids unwrap what God has for them.

Learn to recognize needs.

Kids DO NOT see needs around them. They really don't! Their world is about them, but let's not put blame on them by saying they're selfish and self-centered. Parents and teachers have made them that way. Most families are kid-centered. Restaurants, vacations, and TV programs are chosen because of what the child desires.

Do this exercise. Watch a video–any family-friendly video–together and identify who needs help. Start pointing out needs of the hero and the underdog … and even the villain. Make it a contest to see who can identify the most.

When reading a book, spend time exploring an obvious need. If one of the characters is in a wheelchair, then talk about what that might be like. At first, the kids may think it's an adventure and fun to be in a wheelchair. Direct them, though, to identify with the person in need–in this case, someone in a wheelchair.

- What would you have to ask someone else to do for you?

- What could you not reach?

- What activities/games would you be left out of?

- What view would you have?

Introduce the places where we are presented with needs daily: home, school, church, community, and the world at large. Challenge kids to identify one need in each area once a week. It's hard work at first, but you want them to change their focus, and that takes persistence and practice.

Educate kids on needs. You don't need to depress them! Just give them information. And then, according to their age and abilities, start introducing activities they can be involved in. (We've provided many ideas for you to consider in another part of the book.)

Inform kids about difficult circumstances (hunger, disease, lack of water). This will make them more comfortable early on with people in these situations. Remember the common phrase, "Information is power."

Overcome fear.

The enemy of compassion is fear—a fear of what you don't understand. Did you get that? Say it out loud: The enemy of compassion is fear. Don't be afraid of conversations. Don't be afraid of questions. Don't be afraid of people who are different than you. When you don't understand a situation or why people act like they do, you are afraid of being involved. Eliminating the fear of certain people groups will release you and your kids to show compassion without limits. Kids ask questions because they are curious, not because they have some bias or prejudice formed. Be honest, and they'll grow up treating others with respect.

Twice when our son, Jarad, was young, I was confined to a motorized wheelchair. Other kids thought it looked like a fun thing to play with. Kids we didn't know would approach us in the mall and say things like, "Wow, that looks like fun. Wanna race?" Jarad would get furious and respond with, "Do you think she likes not being able to walk? How would you like it? I wouldn't care if she ran over you!" Our son understood the wheelchair and was not afraid of it. The other kids reacted the way they did because they didn't have knowledge and they were afraid of what the wheelchair represented.

Include LOTS of visuals.

If you're raising money to provide a community well so people can have clean water, then demonstrate how one water treatment packet can clean 10 liters of nasty water (five 2-liter bottles). This type of demonstration shows the desperate need to get clean water to every person.

Use publicity videos from various organizations. Of course, they want your donation, but their videos will most definitely help your kids realize that not everyone in the world lives the way they do.

Label and discuss emotions.

Learning about serving gives kids an opportunity to expand their vocabulary, particularly with words that describe their emotions. Continually ask kids to name their feelings, whether about real people or imaginary situations.

Instead of just using "sad" and "happy" to describe feelings, encourage your kids to identify what they are experiencing more specifically.

- gloomy
- miserable
- unhappy
- pleased
- joyful
- cheerful
- terrified
- glad

- angry
- fuming
- furious
- frightened
- cross
- calm
- depressed
- quiet

Work with your kids to identify a special phrase they can say when they are hurting for someone else–at that unexpected moment when they recognize a need. Say something like: "That breaks my heart." "Make me Your hands and feet, Lord." "God sees and I see."

See the person face-to-face.

Whenever possible, kids need to see the person they are helping face-to-face or at least get an idea of what they look like. This can be through the use of a photo or in a video.

Set up a Compassion Corner at home or in a classroom. Choose a person who is in need—recovering from surgery, just lost a spouse, deployed in the service, lost a job, etc. Set that person's picture on the worktable, along with a description of what his/her situation is. Talk about why the person needs encouragement. What is it he can't do for himself? How could we help? Provide all kinds of craft supplies so the kids can make individual cards for this person. Encourage them to say more than "Get well soon." Think about what you would want someone to say to you. The words you share are extremely important and will be read over and over. Then, put all the cards in a large manila envelope and send them to the person immediately.

> We found that once the person got well, he wanted to reward the kids with treats. This changed the attitude of the kids, so we asked the recipients to receive our gift without reciprocating.

The easiest people to show compassion to are the people who are closest to us—our family and close friends. It's really hard to watch those we love dearly go through a difficult, painful time in their lives. It's not quite as easy to show compassion for someone we don't know or understand ... or maybe don't like. Have kids think about this for a while. Should we serve people who actually hurt us at one time—can we muster up any compassion for them? If the kids have ever experienced a situation like this, it's best to talk about it without a specific needy person in mind. Once the child connects with the situation and the need, then introduce who the person to be served is. It's difficult to turn a needy person away once kids have agreed and felt the need.

Make praying a priority.

Pray for the person as part of the overall servanthood and compassion experience ... not just as something you do when all else fails or you can't think of what to do.

Track the times when you pray for a specific person with something fun that can then be given to the person.

For example, use hot glue to adhere some snack-size candy bars to shish kebob sticks. Each time you pray for that person, add another candy bar flower to a vase. Once you have the vase full, take it to the person. Who could help but be encouraged by a bouquet of candy!

Debrief after every opportunity to serve.

It is imperative that you talk about the servanthood experience immediately following its completion. This helps kids process their feelings and gives them insight into a future plan of action.

Ask these questions:

- Describe what you/we did.

- How did it make you feel to help in that way? Uncomfortable? Happy?

- Why did the person need our help?

- Will that person need help again?

- What caused the problem that meant he/she needed help?

Notice that only one of these questions was a yes/no question. Encourage kids to use descriptive words and develop vocabulary.

Be intentional.

Set a regular time each week or month, so the kids know when you're going to work on a project. They will anticipate the appointment and excitedly talk about their chance to do such-and-such at a particular time.

Developing compassion is akin to developing muscle strength. The more you use your muscles, the stronger they get. When you're going to "exercise" your compassion muscles, recognize it—especially with preschoolers. Teach them the day of the week when you have a regular service project. Preschoolers will come to know Wednesday (or any day you choose) as the day we help somebody. How cool is that!

Make Your Own Muscles!

Make pantyhose muscles for preschoolers. Cut an 8" piece out of the leg of an old pair of pantyhose. Tie a knot in one end. Now, stuff the pantyhose with quilt batting and tie the other end. You'll have something that looks like a squishy potato. When you get ready to exercise your serving muscles, preschoolers can stuff these "muscles" up the sleeves of their shirts.

You also want to be spontaneous about serving, but that comes after a child has had a shift in mindset. If you're not intentional, you'll find that all through life the opportunities slip away. They get taken off the To-Do list. If you've set aside a time and have a plan, it's much more difficult to dismiss serving. Be intentional about things that matter ... and serving others matters.

The result.

When you help kids see that God desires them to serve others, the result will be stories like this one:

The man who had constructed the set for the children's musical was now in the hospital. Having been in many of the children's musicals, fourteen-year-old Bradley knew there was a tremendous amount of behind-the-scenes work to be done—work that doesn't get recognized, but is extremely important nevertheless. He pulled me aside after the musical was over and asked how I intended to get the set taken down. I admitted to him that it was going to be a problem, and I'd have to figure it out by the following day. Bradley said he would speak to his father, but he was sure the two of them could take care of everything. In less than 10 minutes, he returned, asking for specific instructions and assuring me that I didn't have to be concerned about the task any longer. This young man understood the meaning of servanthood and by acting on his understanding became an example to everyone around him.

Awareness
ACTIVITIES

These activities are designed to help children recognize opportunities to serve, realize how quick and easy it can be to help someone, and understand the far-reaching impact servanthood can have.

COLOR TRANSFER

Scripture:

Matthew 25:35-40 (ESV)

"For I was hungry and you gave me food, I was thirsty and you gave me drink, I was a stranger and you welcomed me, I was naked and you clothed me, I was sick and you visited me, I was in prison and you came to me." Then the righteous will answer him, saying, "Lord, when did we see you hungry and feed you, or thirsty and give you drink? And when did we see you a stranger and welcome you, or naked and clothe you? And when did we see you sick or in prison and visit you?" And the King will answer them, "Truly, I say to you, as you did it to one of the least of these my brothers, you did it to me."

You Need

- 4 custard cups
- 3 colors of food coloring
- paper towel
- water
- spoon

Project Instructions

- Fill 3 custard cups about two-thirds full with water. Add 10 drops of one color of food coloring to each cup and stir. Rinse the spoon off in between stirring each color. Now you should have 3 distinct and strong colors of water.

- Position the cups of colored water in a triangle and place the empty custard cup in the middle. The cups of colored water should each be about 3" from the empty one.

- Cut 3 strips of paper towel ½"-1" wide and about 6" long.

- Put one end of one of the strips of paper towel in the empty cup and the other end in one of the cups of colored water. Take a second strip and put one end in the empty cup and the other end in a different cup of colored water. Likewise, with the third strip, put one end in the empty cup and the other end in the last cup of colored water.

- Watch for a minute. Then let the cups set for about 5 minutes.

- The colored water will move through the paper towel strips and fill what was originally an empty cup.

Observation

- How long did it take for the colored water to begin moving into the paper towel when it was placed in the cup?

- How far did the colored water move through the paper towel? Did it stop halfway?

- Describe what the custard cup in the center looked like at the beginning of the experiment.

- Describe what the custard cup in the center looked like after 5 minutes.

- Did we need exactly 3 cups of colored water for this to work?

- How many cups of colored water do you think we could've used?

- What did the water look like in the center custard cup after 5 minutes? What color was it?

Discussion

- Read Matthew 25:35-40. How does this Scripture passage remind you of the experiment we just did? *Don't discount any ideas the kids may come up with and encourage them to think creatively and abstractly. You may even find that their direction is worth exploring or revisiting at another time.*

- Let's say the custard cup in the middle represents someone who has a need. Maybe this is someone who is poor and doesn't have enough money to rent a place for his family to live. All the cups of colored water represent Christ-followers who want to live as God wants them to live. What does this passage of Scripture tell us we should do if we want to follow Christ? *We should help the person who is poor.*

- Thinking about this passage, what would the paper towel represent? *It reminds me of our hands reaching out or when we somehow connect with the person who needs help ... maybe talking with the person and finding out what is happening in his/her life ... maybe being able to help him/her find a place to live or food to eat.*

- Then what would the colored water moving through the paper towel represent? *It's when we actually DO something. It's when we provide a way to help that person and put our words into action.*

- When we reach out to help and serve people, it changes them. The custard cup in the middle was completely empty when we started. This person was hopeless and helpless. The care the people showed—the colored water custard cups—filled this person up. His/Her life changed. When we care for other people because we're grateful that God cares deeply about us, then they change. They're no longer empty, hopeless, and helpless. We are pouring God's love into them by serving them.

- Do you know someone who is hopeless right now? Someone who needs hope? Someone who needs help being filled up?

- Who can you reach out to this week? Name something you can do to pour God's love into someone else.

GIANT RING TOSS

You can purchase a Swimline® Giant Ring Toss set from ToySplash.com for about $40. These awesome inflatable rings are just like the infant plastic toy that has been around for generations. The intended use of the inflatables is as a pool toy, but they work just as well for loads of fun on land. (You could do this activity with the infant toy, but it just doesn't have the same impact.)

Lead the kids in a discussion about different areas where they could serve. Try to come up with 5 areas—one for each of the rings. At the end of your talk-time, you may divide the areas a little differently, but 5 that work well are: family, church, school, community, and world. Use a permanent marker to write one area on each of the inflatable rings.

Indicate a stand-behind line. Start with the largest ring. The kids will take turns telling ways they could serve in the area marked on the largest ring. Each time they name a way that has not been previously mentioned, they get 2 tries at tossing the ring over the post. Once someone has successfully gotten the largest ring to stay on the post, then go to the next largest ring. Have the kids continue contributing ideas in the area marked on that ring. Keep going until you've got all 5 rings in place.

BUILDING WITH PVC

You Need

- random length pieces of ½" PVC pipe
- ½" PVC joints

You will need assorted lengths of PVC that are all the same diameter. Cut the PVC in pieces that are between 6" to 12" long. Also, you'll need matching sized PVC joints. Give each child a length of PVC or a PVC joint.

Say:

We want to be compassionate people who "do what we can" to help others. (*The leader will point to a child with a piece of PVC and a child with a PVC joint while saying the next part.*) If you are a compassionate person and do what you can to help in a needy situation, (*point to one child*) and if you are a compassionate person who is willing to do what you can in a needy situation (*point to the other child*), then together you're going to make a difference–a bigger difference. You're going to get something accomplished. (*Join their pieces of PVC. Point to another child who is holding a piece of PVC.*) Now, if you decide you're going to do what you can do in this needy situation, you can join with these others to get more accomplished. (*Connect this piece to the PVC joint.*) We're getting somewhere now!

(*Give a signal and all the kids will find a place to attach their piece of PVC or the PVC joint they have been given. In the end, all the pieces should be joined together in some fashion.*) Wow! Look what all those little pieces became. When we all have compassion and contribute what we can, we can accomplish a lot!

FAMILY SERVICE STATIONS

This is an event where families work together at different stations and move at their own speed. A 2-hour timeframe works well, and because they are working at their own speed, if they come late or have to leave early, it doesn't have a huge impact on the event.

You will need to set up the supplies for at least 6 different projects families could do together. You can also think of these as learning centers. Each project should be in a different room, so no one is distracted by what is going on elsewhere. During the allotted time, families will complete something they will use in the near future to serve someone. Here are some starter ideas for the stations, but don't feel you have to use only these. Come up with your own family serving ideas!

- Make sandwiches to distribute to the homeless.
- Create cards to deliver to a nursing home.
- Make holiday decorations for a family shelter.
- Spend 30 minutes cleaning out the church barn, a closet, or some area of the church.
- Make soup-in-a-bag (This is where all the dry ingredients are put in a bag, so the recipient only needs to add hot water. Various recipes for these can be found online.)
- Make some Rolo® Pretzels for a public servant (nurses, policemen, garbage collectors, firemen).

Recipe for Rolo® Pretzels

Ingredients:

- Rolo® candies
- pretzel knots
- pecan halves
- flat microwavable pan
- parchment paper
- microwave

Cover a flat microwavable pan with parchment paper. Place the pretzel knots on the pan with about 1" between them. There doesn't need to be much space. Unwrap Rolo® chocolate-caramel candies and position one in the center of each pretzel knot. Place the sheet in the microwave. You'll need to experiment with your microwave, but it should take 20-30 seconds to soften the candies.

As soon as the pan comes out of the microwave, press a pecan half into the softened Rolo®. You can leave them out to cool or put them in the freezer to cool quickly. Once they are completely cool, package them in ziplock bags or tins that you can purchase at a dollar store.

TEACH KIDS TO JUMP!

We often notice that someone needs help, and then we look around to see who's going to step forward ... or maybe we just continue to watch the person awkwardly trying to do something. Hey! I don't think that's what Jesus had in mind when He told us to serve one another.

You're the one who can help right now. It doesn't have to be something you plan and prepare for. Just open your eyes; then move your feet! People will talk about how a young person stepped up and helped them without being coerced or told to. It just takes a willing heart.

Jump up when you see ways to serve!

You've probably already seen these ways you could JUMP up:

- Help someone struggling to put on or take off a coat
- Take a grocery cart to the return station for someone
- Hold the door open for someone
- At the very moment, verbally share your praise and gratitude to God when you notice how He is working in your situation.
- Apologize quickly. Don't think about it, get to feeling more and more guilty, and then wander back to apologize (or worse, just think it will blow over).
- Compliment people (maybe a total stranger) on what they're wearing, on their haircut, or their child.
- Offer your seat to someone–on a bus, waiting in the doctor's office, or waiting for a table at a restaurant.
- Offer to help a neighbor who is working out in the yard.
- Readily say "Thank You" so people immediately around the other person hear.
- Be the first to smile!

25 PROJECT IDEAS *for* SERVING

BIRTHDAY PARTY

Scripture:

Psalm 118:24 (NLT)
This is the day the Lord has made.
We will rejoice and be glad in it.

You Need

- leftover birthday decorations
- birthday supplies
- balloons
- cake
- birthday plates
- party games
- gifts
- construction paper
- markers
- individual presents

What You Are Doing

The kids will be providing a birthday party for children living at a women's or family shelter. Many of your kids will have a difficult time understanding that there are children who don't have their own personal birthday party every year. Some kids NEVER get this experience! Deliver all the makings for a birthday party to a family shelter, and give one big party for ALL the kids there! It doesn't matter when the children's birthdays actually are–celebrate them all together.

Who You Are Serving

You will be serving kids who are in temporary housing and who may never have received the attention of a birthday party. This gives them a few moments to experience that special feeling of having a celebration in their honor.

Project Instructions

- This may be a situation where your group will not be allowed to actually serve people face-to-face. Kids who are in family shelters may very well be fellow classmates, but they've chosen to keep their situation private. You can imagine the reaction of discovering a classmate in a shelter. Many shelters have policies that prevent "outside" kids from coming in, so check with your local shelter before proceeding.

- Someone is always having a birthday party! And, most of the time, there are leftover supplies or reusable ones. You can actually work on this project year-round and ask the kids to contribute whatever is left over from their own parties or from ones they attend. This includes everything from napkins to prizes to crepe paper to table coverings. It also includes every kind of theme: pirate, princess, superheroes, trains, whatever. Then, when you are ready to move forward with this project, you will already have lots of supplies.

- Ask the shelter to provide the first name and age of each child there. Make a personal birthday card for each child at the shelter.

- Have each kid in your group choose one of the children and bring a wrapped gift to the party for that child.

- Go through all the supplies and choose what you want to use.

- Discuss with the kids what makes up a good party and then plan accordingly.

- Provide a birthday cake—either one the kids make together, a purchased one, or one someone in the church makes. If possible, write the name of each child in the shelter on the cake.

- Provide some fun, easy-to-set-up games. The kids can choose which ones they'd like to include, but remind them of the age span, so they can choose age-appropriately. Encourage your kids to make the kids at the shelter feel special by celebrating their turn at the games and insisting they go first.

- If you are not allowed to be at the party, then you can put all the supplies and gifts in a box and deliver it. When it comes to a cake, don't send a box mix and icing, because the recipients may not have cooking facilities available to them. Send a premade cake.

Discussion

- How many of you had a birthday party of some kind on your last birthday? It may have been with friends or with your family ... or some of you may have had both! You may be surprised to know that there are lots of kids who never have a birthday party and never receive a birthday present. Their family's financial situation is rough, and they struggle to have a place to sleep and food to eat, so doing something extravagant and costly like having a birthday party isn't something they can do.

- Read Psalm 118:24 together. *Say it aloud together a couple of times, but substitute "birthday" for "day."* Does it feel different when you say the Bible verse that way? How does it connect with our birthday party project?

- Why do people have to stay in family or women's shelters? *Talk about the loss of a job, the lack of extended family who can help, or the need to get away from abusive situations.*

- What are some of the things you would feel or think about if your family faced living in a shelter?

- Birthday parties are not something you have to have in order to survive. So how is giving a birthday party serving others? How is that serving God?

- What was your favorite part of the birthday party? If we did this again, what could we do differently to make it even better?

Ten women were seated at a table, deep in discussion about teaching kids to serve, when I mentioned the idea of giving a birthday party at a shelter. Most of them were surprised that this was a need, and they couldn't imagine that a child wouldn't have his/her birthday recognized. Then my eyes locked with the young woman sitting directly across from me—her eyes filled to the brim with tears. When I asked if she was okay, her reply pierced all our hearts. "It wasn't until I was married that I had my first birthday party. My mother-in-law made a big deal of my birthday, and it took our relationship to a brand new level. She really did care about me."

BOO-BOO BASKET

Scripture:

Luke 10:34 (NIV) ***(See also, the Parable of the Good Samaritan, Luke 10:25-37)***

He went to him and bandaged his wounds, pouring on oil and wine. Then he put the man on his own donkey, brought him to an inn and took care of him.

You Need

- small basket
- first aid cream
- Band-Aids®
- gauze
- washcloth
- elastic bandage
- cotton swabs
- antiseptic towelettes
- small scissors
- large Band-Aid®
- permanent marker

What You Are Doing

The kids will be preparing a basket(s) of first aid supplies.

Who You Are Serving

These first aid, Boo-Boo Baskets can be something the children make for their family, for a classroom, for a team, or any place where small groups of children meet. The baskets can also be given to family shelters, people who do home childcare, office workers, traveling sales reps, etc. They would make wonderful kits to send with people going on mission trips. In that case, though, it would be best to put the supplies in a plastic container with a snap-on lid.

The Boo-Boo Basket should be placed in a location everyone knows about and can easily access.

Project Instructions

- When someone says they have a boo-boo, what do they mean? They mean they have an injury, a cut, or a scrape that probably needs some attention. Boo-boos are small injuries that generally happen when kids (or adults) are not paying attention or are moving too quickly. When a boo-boo happens, you need something to help take care of it. We're going to make a kit that will be available when those boo-boos happen.

- Decide for whom you are going to make the baskets and how many you will need. This will keep you from purchasing too many supplies and will also confirm that each child will get to participate.

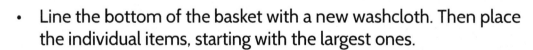

- You will need a small basket for each first aid kit you put together. You could also use small plastic containers with snap-on lids.

- Collect all kinds of first aid items. Make sure they are new. If you're making several kits, buy large boxes of each item and divide them into smaller amounts in sandwich bags.

- Line the bottom of the basket with a new washcloth. Then place the individual items, starting with the largest ones.

- Make a label out of a large Band-Aid®. Use a permanent marker to write "BOO-BOO BASKET First Aid Kit" on it. Adhere the label to the basket either by sticking it on (if there is a nice smooth surface) or by leaving the paper on the back and tying it to the basket. You will need a hole punch and ribbon if tying it on.

- The kids should be part of distributing the baskets to the places that were in the initial plans. Do not deliver the baskets for them! Their interaction with the groups they are serving is very important.

Discussion

- When do you think one of these baskets might be needed?

- What should happen if the injury is worse than these supplies can take care of?

- When have you had a boo-boo and needed something from the Boo-Boo Basket?

- Talk about the Parable of the Good Samaritan from Luke 10:25-37.

- Read Luke 10:34 (from the parable). How do you think the Samaritan took care of the injured man? What kind of supplies do you think he had?

- How have we served others through this project?

CARE PACKAGES

Scripture:

Philippians 1:3 (NLT)

Every time I think of you, I give thanks to my God.

You Need

- small USPS flat rate shipping boxes
- small candies
- miscellaneous small items (toys, school supplies, party favors)
- hometown postcards
- addresses of freshmen college students
- markers
- construction paper
- copies of greeting card

What You Are Doing

The kids will be preparing and shipping care packages to freshmen college students.

Who You Are Serving

About 6 weeks after young people leave for their freshman year at college, many of them start to miss the familiar things of home. In this project, the kids will send a care package full of silly things and goodies to cheer up these college freshmen and remind them that someone at home is thinking of them.

Project Instructions

- Prepare the USPS flat rate shipping boxes by putting them together and addressing each one to a college freshman. This way, the kids will be able to identify a box of someone they know particularly well.

- Challenge the kids to bring in small items to include in the care package. These could include school supplies/stationary items and small toys.

(Even though you may question it, college students love little wind-up toys, Slinkies®, kazoos, glow-in-the-dark sticks, and such.)

- On the opposite side of the box from the addressed side, the kids will use markers to write Philippians 1:3, *Every time I think of you, _____ (name of recipient), I give thanks to my God.* This side can be decorated with drawings and patterns.

- When the scripture and drawings are completed, stand the boxes up so the open end is easy to access.

- The kids will place the items they brought in the boxes. If they brought a package of mechanical pencils, then they can open the package and put one pencil in each box. Continue putting items in the boxes until everything has been distributed.

- If you have a popular tourist attraction in your town, include a hometown postcard in the care box just for fun and remembrance.

- Beforehand, the leader should run off copies of a card (see the sample at the end of this project) that identifies whom the care package is from. Take time for the kids to individually sign their first name to each of the cards. Then insert one into each box.

- If the boxes still need more added to them, the leader can do that afterwards. Otherwise, remove the tape strips and close the boxes.

- Mail the boxes the next day, if at all possible.

Discussion

- How do you think the college students will react when they open the box?

- Being away from home for the very first time, all on your own, brings a student many new experiences. What would freshmen college students need to learn to do on their own? What would they have to do that their parents usually took care of? Who do you think they are missing back home?

- What were the recipients of the boxes reminded of before they even opened the box? *Whoever handled or saw the box would've seen Philippians 1:3. They would know that someone was thinking about them.* How does it make you feel when you know someone is thinking of you and thanking God that they know you? *Pretty awesome!*

- How are these boxes an act of serving someone? Are the items something the college students need? *Not really. What they need is a reminder of home.*

- Who else would a box like this cheer up?

Possible Wording for Greeting Card: **(or simply photocopy the next page)**

> We hope you are having a wonderful time getting used to a new life at college. We're sure you're meeting lots of new friends and enjoying new experiences. You are missed here, and we wanted you to know. So we got together and made this care package especially for you. Enjoy it!
> We hope it makes you smile.

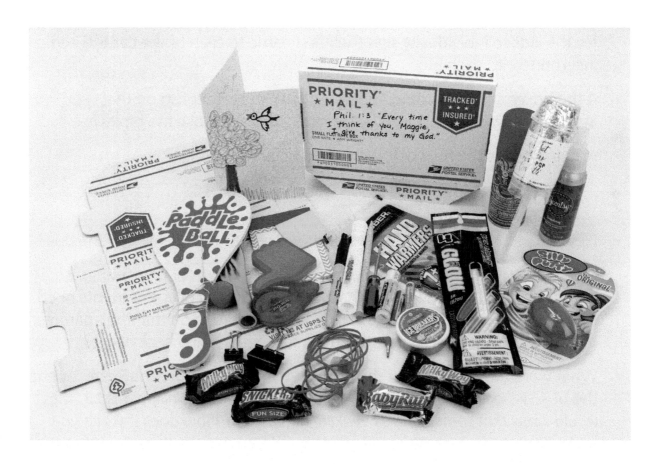

Hello!

We hope you are having a wonderful time getting used to a new life at college. We're sure you're meeting lots of new friends and enjoying new experiences. You are missed here, and we wanted you to know. So we got together and made this care package especially for you.

Enjoy it!

We hope it makes you smile.

CASSEROLES ON CALL

Scripture:

Psalm 30:2 (NASB)

O Lord my God, I cried to You for help, and You healed me.

You Need

- ingredients for casserole recipe
- vacuum sealer
- vacuum sealing bags
- 9" x 9" foil pans
- nonstick cooking spray
- freezer space
- foil
- permanent marker

What You Are Doing

The kids will mass-produce casseroles that can be vacuum-sealed and frozen until they are needed.

Who You Are Serving

The casseroles will be "on call" and ready to pull out of the freezer anytime they are needed. These are especially helpful when someone is recovering from a foot or leg injury/surgery and having difficulty getting around. Also, people who live by themselves, recovering from any kind of illness, could use a meal. They may not have anyone to even go out and grab a fast food meal. You have no idea how valuable a casserole is until you've been on the receiving end of one! It's a lifesaver!

Project Instructions

- Decide which recipe you will be making and purchase the ingredients. If possible, take 2 of the kids with you on the shopping trip, just so they can have the experience. Next time you do this project take 2 different kids. A few recipes have been provided for you, but feel free to use your favorite.

- Set up an area as an assembly line. We're going to describe making the chicken casserole, but you can do a similar set-up with any recipe you decide on. Since cooking the chicken and the pasta require waiting, prepare these ahead of time.

  Stations:

  - chop or pull apart cooked chicken into small pieces
  - measure and mix seasonings
  - combine seasonings with soups
  - combine chicken, soup mixture, pasta, and vegetables
  - spray pans, fill with combined ingredients, and cover with foil

- Make sure everyone washes up before beginning any food preparation.

- The recipe will make more than enough to fill a 9" x 9" pan, but duplicate the recipe multiple times to make a large supply of casseroles. Save any extra for the next pan.

- Once the pans are filled and covered in foil, place them in the freezer overnight. DO NOT cook the casseroles before freezing.

- The frozen casseroles can be popped out of the foil pans and inserted into vacuum seal bags. The foil pans can be washed and used several times before losing their shape.

- Vacuum seal the bag. Using a permanent marker, write the name of the casserole and the date it was packaged.

- Stack the casseroles in a freezer.

- Anytime someone is in need of a meal, pull out a frozen casserole, open the bag, and place it in a foil pan to thaw. (Do not thaw in the vacuum seal bag or it will be difficult to get out.) If you want to deliver it warm, then bake the thawed casserole (uncovered) at 350° for 30 minutes. Or, you can deliver it thawed with instructions on how to warm it. Taking it in the foil pan keeps the person from having to remember to return a dish.

- Encourage the kids to watch for people who may need a meal. They can suggest names. Even more important than making the casserole is being part of the delivery. The kids can take turns going with you to give this gift. Remember that the person is healing, so don't stay long. Ask how they are doing, and offer to get out any plates, silverware, or napkins that would help.

Discussion

- Read Psalm 30:2. What is the person doing in this verse?

- How does God sometimes provide His help? *He uses His people to show His love. By helping people who are recovering from an illness or surgery, we are demonstrating God's healing love.*

- What was good about making a large supply of the casseroles?

- Put yourself in the place of someone receiving a casserole. How do you think you would feel? What if you were the one responsible for feeding your family? *When you're recovering from surgery, you still want to do what you've always done, but your body needs time and rest to heal. You feel guilty for not being able to take care of your family, even though they can do things for themselves. Providing a casserole helps the recovering person feel like they have kept their responsibility.*

- Describe your experience when you delivered a casserole.

RECIPES

Baked Spaghetti

- 8 oz. spaghetti
- ½ c. margarine
- 1 egg, beaten
- 1 c. Parmesan cheese
- 1 c. cottage cheese
- ½ onion, diced
- 1 lb. hamburger, browned and drained
- large jar of spaghetti sauce
- ⅛ t. oregano
- ⅛ t. garlic salt
- 1½ c. mozzarella cheese

Cook the spaghetti and drain. Combine the spaghetti, beaten egg, butter, and Parmesan cheese. Brown the hamburger with the diced onion and drain off the fat. Sprinkle the oregano and garlic salt into the meat and stir.

Lightly butter the bottom of the pan. Pour in the cooked spaghetti to make the bottom layer. Spread the cottage cheese next, then half the mozzarella cheese, browned hamburger, and a layer of spaghetti sauce. Top with the rest of the mozzarella cheese.

Bake uncovered at 350° for 30 minutes.

Cheesy Polska Kielbasa

- 1 pkg. polska kielbasa
- 1 can cream of celery soup
- 1½ c. milk
- 1½ c. pasta (penne, elbows, pinwheels, etc.)
- 1½ c. french-fried onions
- 1 c. shredded cheddar, mild
- 1 c. green beans, frozen or canned (or other vegetable)

Slice polska kielbasa into ¼" slices and lightly brown them in a skillet.

Combine the soup and the milk. Then stir in the cooked pasta, polska kielbasa, green beans, french-fried onions, and the cheddar cheese.

Bake covered at 375° for 45 minutes.

Chicken and Pasta Casserole

- 1½ c. dry pasta
- 4 chicken breasts
- 1 T. dried minced onion
- ⅛ t. salt
- ⅛ t. pepper
- ⅛ t. garlic
- 1 T. dried basil
- 1 T. dried and crushed parsley
- 1 can cream of chicken soup
- 1 can of cream of mushroom soup
- 1½ c. frozen mixed vegetables

Cook the dried pasta in boiling water until al dente. Don't overcook. Drain the pasta.

Boil the chicken breasts for 6 minutes. Let them cool and then cut them into small pieces. (You may want to have the chicken cooked and cooled before getting the kids together.)

Mix the salt, pepper, garlic, basil, parsley, and onion together. Combine the seasonings with both cans of soup. Then, in a large bowl, combine the chicken, soup mixture, vegetables, and the pasta.

Spray a foil pan with non-stick cooking spray and fill the pan.

Bake uncovered at 350° for 30 minutes.

CLEAN WATER

Scripture:

John 4:13-14 (NLT)

Jesus replied, "Anyone who drinks this water will soon become thirsty again. But those who drink the water I give will never be thirsty again. It becomes a fresh, bubbling spring within them, giving them eternal life."

You Need

- 5 2-liter bottles (empty or full)
- empty water bottles
- labels
- packing tape

What You Are Doing

You will be educating the kids on the worldwide need for clean water. Then they will be participating in a project to raise money to help with this desperate situation.

Who You Are Serving

The kids will be serving people who have no clean drinking water and have to walk for miles to get a bucket of dirty water. As a result of not having clean water, these people—many of them children—die of all kinds of diseases.

Project Instructions

- Go to the website **csdw.org**, sponsored by Proctor & Gamble, and watch the video called "Help Provide Clean Drinking Water." It is less than a minute in length, but demonstrates how one small, inexpensive packet can transform 10 liters of filthy water into clean water. Show the kids 5 2-liter bottles. This is how much water one packet cleans.

- Although you can use the information from the **csdw.org** site to educate the children, we recommend you contribute the funds you raise to one of the many organizations that provide clean water in the name of our Lord Jesus.

- Now watch the video called "The Water Effect" on the World Vision website, **worldvision.org**. It's about 3 minutes in length and provides information on why clean water is so important. World Vision provides clean water through building wells. There are several ways we can reach the goal of every child having clean water to drink.

- Facts to know:

  - A child under 5 dies about every minute as a result of diarrhea caused by contaminated water. ("#Water Effect")
  - Nearly 1,600 children will die each day because of a lack of clean water, sanitation, and hygiene. ("New Sesame Street Muppet...")

- Make a collection container. Give each child 2 labels. One label will have the 2 facts printed on it. The other label will have John 4:13-14 written out. They will place these labels on empty water bottles. Use some clear packing tape to cover the labels so they are secure.

- Encourage the kids to collect DIMES in this container. Other coins will not fit ... but they could also take dollar bills. Dimes are also easy for kids of any age to count—1, 2, 3, 4, 5, 6, 7, 8, 9, 10!

- Brainstorm with the kids where they might be able to collect dimes—car seats, Grandma's couch ... just keep your eyes open.

- Their best tool for collecting dimes from other people is being informed about the water situation. Provide websites and brochures where the kids can collect information on their own.

- Repeatedly review the facts on what a difference providing water can make in a child's life.

  - They feel better, so they can study and get a better education.
  - They won't die from diseases caused by filthy water.
  - They are happier because they feel better.
  - They can help provide for their families.

- When Collection Day arrives, celebrate by having the kids make stacks of 10 dimes ... everywhere! Write in GIANT numbers how many stacks have been counted as the kids fill a table or square on the floor.

- If the organization you are donating the money to has a dollar amount that provides "X" amount of water, then let your older kids do the math. Figure out how much clean water you were able to provide by the number of dimes you collected.

A child carried his water bottle to school and set it on his desk each day. He came to me on collection day and said that he needed more water bottles. I asked him, "How many?" He said, "I'm not really sure." Then he dragged in two grocery bags loaded with dimes. When I asked him how he had collected so many, he said that when his teacher saw the bottle on his desk day after day, she went through the coins she had been saving for a vacation and pulled out all the dimes. You never know whose heart will be touched by a specific need!

Discussion

- How did it make you feel when you watched the video that showed the nasty water people drink every day? How does the water get so dirty?

- Turn on a faucet and stick your face under the flow of water. Do you appreciate the water a little more now?

- What did you think when you saw how quickly the nasty water could be made clean with one little packet? Would you feel okay about drinking the water after it had gone through the process with the packet? Would you still be a little afraid to drink it? Why?

- How does providing people with clean drinking water spread the message of Jesus our Savior? *When people know you truly care about them, they will listen to your message. Christian organizations not only set up wells and provide packets for cleaning water, they get to share about the Living Water–Jesus.*

- Why do we call Jesus "the Living Water"? *God created people to need Him in their lives–like they're really thirsty for Him. People try to live without God, but it just doesn't work. It's like they drank something, but they're still thirsty. It didn't satisfy them. If we believe in Jesus, then that part of us that only God can satisfy is taken care of. Our thirst is quenched. As long as we believe and rely on Jesus as our Savior and Lord, we won't need other things to try to fill that place. Jesus will quench that thirst.*

- Read John 4:13-14. When we provide clean drinking water, we provide people with something they desperately need physically. Then, when we tell those people about Jesus the Living Water, we provide them with something they desperately need spiritually. See how that goes together? Amazing!

- Why do you think it pleases God when we get clean water to the kids who need it?

COMPASSION CENTER

Scripture:

1 Peter 3:8 (NIV)
Finally, all of you, be like-minded, be sympathetic, love one another, be compassionate and humble.

You Need

- construction paper
- stickers
- art supplies
- index cards
- photo of person
- large manila envelope

What You Are Doing

The kids will be making cards of encouragement. This is a good activity to set up on the first Sunday of every month for the kids to engage in as they arrive. It's one of my favorite "Mosey In" activities.

Who You Are Serving

Choose someone in your church to be your focus for the Compassion Center. People who would be a good choice for this are those recovering from an accident or illness, or someone going through a loss.

Project Instructions

- Set up a table with construction paper, stickers, markers, crayons, scissors, glue sticks, and other art supplies. Place this table off to the side (or in a corner) away from the main teaching area. You can hang a sign over the table that identifies it as the Compassion Center.

- Choose someone from your church who will be the focus of the Compassion Center. Post a picture of that person at the table. If you have a church directory, this is a good place to locate the photo. The photo is very important because it gives the children a face to identify with. The activity has exponentially more impact when this photo is present.

- Write on an index card what the person's situation is right now that makes them the candidate for the Compassion Center. Just give brief information; don't go into details.

- Address a large manila envelope to the person and place this envelope next to the photo.

- The kids will design individual cards for this person. Encourage them to write a note that is more than "Get Well" or "Hope you are feeling better." The pictures they draw are nice, but the person receiving the cards will savor the ones with more detailed messages … over and over.

- When time is up, place all the cards in the large manila envelope.

- The very next day, make sure this is dropped in the mail.

Discussion

- What does it mean to be compassionate?

- Read together 1 Peter 3:8. How are these cards a way we can live out this scripture?

- What challenges do you think this person is facing right now in his/her situation?

- How do you think people receiving the cards will react when they open the big envelope? How will that change their day?

- Is there anything else we could do for this person to show compassion?

- Are there some people we have spotlighted in the Compassion Center who you connected with more than others? Why is that?

One of the things that is likely to happen is that once the person who received the cards is well, he or she will want to bring a treat for the kids to express gratitude. Although this is a really nice gesture, discourage the person from doing that. When gifts become a regular thing, the children start to expect to receive a reward for showing compassion. You want them to realize they serve others in obedience to God. The gratification comes from knowing you did what God wanted you to do, not to get a sucker or a cupcake.

COOKIES FOR TRUCK DRIVERS

Scripture:

Deuteronomy 31:8 (NASB)

*The Lord is the one who goes ahead of you;
He will be with you. He will not fail you or
forsake you. Do not fear or be dismayed.*

You Need

- ingredients for easy-to-make homemade cookies
- copies of Deuteronomy 31:8
- supplies to make cards
- long stick (broom handle)

What You Are Doing

This is an excellent serving idea for families to do together and incorporate into their traveling, especially at Christmas time. The kids will be making cookies to give away to truckers at rest areas.

Who You Are Serving

Have you ever been on your way to Grandma's house on Christmas Eve and noticed how full of semi-trucks the rest areas are? These drivers are out on the road, making sure gifts are on the store shelves and food is at the grocery. They must miss being with their families. You don't have to limit yourself to the Christmas season to do this project, though, because truck drivers are away from home throughout the year.

Project Instructions

- Choose an easy-to-make cookie recipe.

- If possible, take the kids with you to purchase the ingredients.

- Have fun making cookies together.

- Once the cookies have cooled completely, package them in ziplock bags.

- While you're waiting for the cookies to cool, make some special cards to let the truckers know you're thinking of them, praying for them, and that God loves them.

- Include a card with each package of cookies, along with a tag that has Deuteronomy 31:8 written out on it.

- When you're on the road, take a few minutes to pull off in a rest area to personally deliver the cookies. Take a long stick (like a broom handle) with you to attach the bag of cookies to and raise it up to the semi's window. Both the kids and truckers will get a kick out of that!

Discussion

- Read Deuteronomy 31:8. Why do you think this verse would be an encouragement to truckers? Do you think they ever get afraid when the weather turns bad? How do you think they feel when their truck breaks down? What do you think is going through their minds when they have to miss their child's birthday because they're out on the road?

- Why do you think these truck drivers would appreciate our cookie gift?

- What would be difficult about being on the road for days at a time, all year long? *Being by yourself can be lonely, especially when everyone else is going to parties and enjoying friends. God wants to be our forever companion. He wants to be close to us and go through every moment of life with us. When we accept Jesus as our Savior and become God's forever children, He is always with us, and we're not really ever alone.*

- What was the reaction of the truckers you gave cookies to?

- How do you think our act of service changed this day for the truckers?

E-MAIL A MISSIONARY

Scripture:

Luke 24:46 (NLT)

And he said, "Yes, it was written long ago that the Messiah would suffer and die and rise from the dead on the third day. It was also written that this message would be proclaimed in the authority of his name to all the nations, beginning in Jerusalem: 'There is forgiveness of sins for all who repent.'"

You Need

- access to a computer
- leader's e-mail account
- missionary's e-mail address
- photo of missionary (and his/her family)

What You Are Doing

The kids will be putting together a delightful and inquisitive e-mail.

Who You Are Serving

The e-mail will be sent to a missionary and has several objectives. First of all, it is meant to be an encouragement for the work the missionary is doing. Secondly, it will prove to be an educational tool for the children as they receive direct information about the particular mission field where this missionary serves.

Project Instructions

- If your church sponsors a missionary, the missionary likely has provided a pamphlet or some kind of information piece about his/her family and the work they are involved in. Gather as much information as you can.

- Set up a photo of the missionary and his/her family.

- Talk to the children about what you've found out about this missionary from reading the information provided.

- Set up a computer with the missionary's e-mail address entered.

- Beforehand, enter all the prompting questions into the body of the e-mail, and then give each child a copy of them. The kids will look over these questions to decide what they would like to personally say in the e-mail.

- You can handle the e-mail in one of two ways. The leader can sit at the computer and enter the things each child would like to say, including his/her first name and age with each response. Or, the kids can take turns at the keyboard to respond on their own. When the leader enters the responses, the kids will usually say more. When they enter information themselves, they get tired and make their comments very brief. You could also do a mixture of both. The kids can answer as many or as few of the questions as they prefer.

- After they have told about themselves, end the e-mail with questions they would like to ask the missionary. This will prompt the missionary to return the e-mail and provide particular kids with specific answers.

- Gather everyone who has contributed around the computer. Pray for the missionary and the work they are doing. Then push the "Send" button together.

Discussion

- Read together Luke 24:46. How does this verse help you understand what a missionary does and why he/she does it?

- Missionaries are far from home. What do you think they miss? Why is it important that we share things about ourselves with them?

- How do you think our e-mail was able to help this missionary?

- What do you think you could learn by writing this missionary on a regular basis?

- Was this difficult? Did it cost us a lot of money? What did it cost us?
  A little time is all. Even though we may not have money to give, we can serve others with words of encouragement–by setting aside a few minutes of our time and stepping into the opportunity.

Prompting Questions

- Tell about something silly you did with your family.

- What's your favorite thing about school?

- What's your favorite Bible story? Why?

- What do you like to do in your spare time?

- When have you felt closest to God?

- Where have you been on vacation?

- What do you like to do during the summer?

- Tell about a time when someone helped you or when you helped someone else.

- If you could live anywhere in the world, where would you like to live?

- What question would you like to ask God?

- What question would you like to ask _____ (name of missionary)?

    Such as: What's the hardest thing about being a missionary? When did you know that God wanted you to be a missionary?

Additional ideas:

FAMILY SCAVENGER HUNT

Scripture:

Matthew 19:21 (NIV)

Jesus answered, "If you want to be perfect, go, sell your possessions and give to the poor, and you will have treasure in heaven. Then come, follow me."

You Need

- copies of the Family Discard and Donate Scavenger Hunt list
- pencils
- large container (box, laundry basket, tub) for each family member

What You Are Doing

The entire family will be going on a scavenger hunt to find items to throw away or donate. You only have 30 minutes, so make your decisions quickly.

Who You Are Serving

This project makes it possible to serve in multiple ways. The things you choose to donate will help those who can't afford to purchase "extra" items. At the same time, you're serving your family by discarding unnecessary things that are cluttering up the house.

Project Instructions

- Give each person a copy of the Family Discard and Donate Scavenger Hunt list. If you have nonreaders in your family, then an adult can tell them 1 or 2 things on the list at a time.

- Each person will need his/her own area to put the things he/she has gathered. You will want to provide a box, laundry basket, or some sort of large container for each person.

- Set a timer for 30 minutes. When the timer is started, everyone will take a list and try to locate items that can be discarded, but the items must belong to that person. You cannot discard something that belongs to someone else!

- As each item is decided upon, it is placed in that person's container. Once it has gone in the container, there's no going back. You have given it away.

- When the timer goes off, compare how many things you were able to check off your list.

Discussion

- How did you feel about deciding what to give away so quickly?

- Which item was the most difficult to give away?

- Which item was the easiest?

- What things did you have an abundance of—more than you need?

- How can you decide when it's time to give clothes away? Are they the correct size for you? Have you worn them this past year?

- Did you choose canned and boxed foods that you like or dislike? If they were things you dislike, were you really giving up anything?

- What type of things did you feel most comfortable donating?

- Read Matthew 19:16-23. This is the story we often call "The Rich Young Ruler." He followed all the commandments and wanted to know what else he needed to do to get into heaven. What Jesus told him didn't make him very happy. Why was it so difficult for the man to do what Jesus told him to do? How are we like this man?

- How do you think this exercise will change the way you look at your "stuff" in the future?

Family Discard & Donate Scavenger Hunt List

- [ ] Choose a shirt, T-shirt, or other top.

- [ ] Choose an accessory (belt, earrings, bracelet, ribbon, hat, scarf, etc.)

- [ ] Choose a toy, puzzle, or game (that is not broken).

- [ ] Find 2 things that need to be thrown away but aren't in the garbage yet.

- [ ] Choose a can of food.

- [ ] Choose a pair of pants.

- [ ] Choose a food that comes in a box.

- [ ] Find something in any drawer that you can donate.

- [ ] Choose a book to give away.

- [ ] Choose a DVD or CD to give away.

- [ ] Choose a holiday decoration—any holiday.

- [ ] Donate one thing of your choice!

FAMILY VAN

Scripture:

Exodus 20:12 (NIV)

Honor your father and your mother, so that you may live long in the land the Lord your God is giving you.

You Need

- garbage can
- handheld vacuum cleaner
- sanitary wet wipes
- empty container/bag/box

What You Are Doing

The kids will be cleaning out the family van. The family could also do this together, but it would be best for the kid(s) to take this on as their own project.

Who You Are Serving

In our busy world, the family van gets lived in and ends up filled with school paper, empty fast food containers, and dirty socks. What a mess! And it's everybody's mess. There's no one person who contributed all of it. The kids will serve their parents by volunteering to clean out the family van.

Project Instructions

- When cleaning out the van, no one is allowed to claim whose mess it is and only clean up the part he/she made. You're doing this to honor your parents because they provide you with transportation to so many places.

- Throw out all garbage. Don't forget to look under the seats.

- Put anything that needs to go back in the house to be put away in a container. If there's a question whether it's to be thrown out or kept, it's best to put it in the container and ask. Then, when everything is in the container that goes in the house, don't just take the container in. Put everything away!

- Use some sanitary wipes to clean out cup holders, the steering wheel, shoe prints on the back of seats, and anywhere else that needs a shine.

- Remove the floor mats and wash them off. Also, clean the carpet underneath.

- Use a handheld vacuum to clean all carpeted areas. Don't forget to use the anteater nozzle to get down in those tight places.

Discussion

- How did your parents react when they saw the clean van?

- Read Exodus 20:12. How are you living out this scripture by doing this project?

- Who were you serving in this project? *Your parents, of course, but also the entire family and whomever you give a ride to. They will all enjoy a nice clean van! Life is hectic, and this is one chore that many times gets put off to another day. What a nice way to show you appreciate what your parents do!*

- Is there anything you would change about the way you did this to make it easier next time?

- What could you do to honor your parents every time you ride in the van? *Maybe you could set a personal goal always to check to make sure you are taking your things out of the van with you when you return home. Cleaning won't seem like such a big job if you remember to serve your family every time you head out in the van.*

FUNKY FRUIT BASKETS

Scripture:

2 John 1:12 (ESV)

Though I have much to write to you, I would rather not use paper and ink. Instead I hope to come to you and talk face to face, so that our joy may be complete.

You Need

- different kinds of fruit
- baskets
- wiggle eyes
- craft glue
- permanent markers
- doll accessories (hats, earrings)
- lace
- Easter grass or shredded paper
- scrub brushes
- dry towels

What You Are Doing

The kids will be making and delivering baskets of funky fruit–fruit that they've decorated to look like heads. They are similar to Mr. Potato Head, only using different fruits and mostly drawn-on faces.

Who You Are Serving

These funky fruit baskets will be taken to people who live in an assisted living facility and delivered during a mealtime when they are all together.

Project Instructions

- The kids will bring 3 or 4 pieces of fruit with them to contribute to the baskets.

- Gather some small baskets from yard sales to use in arranging the completed fruit.

- Show the kids how to scrub each piece of fruit with a scrub brush under running water (not a tub of water and don't use soap). Dry the fruit completely once cleaning is done. Getting the fruit nice and clean is not only safer to eat but will help in being able to get the decorations to stick.

- Provide the kids with wiggle eyes, doll accessories, and permanent markers. (Water-based markers will not work on the fruit skins.) They will decorate each piece of fruit to look like a face. Encourage them to make silly and happy faces ... nothing scary. The kids will have a blast doing this!

- Put some Easter grass or shredded paper in the bottom of each basket as a base.

- Fill each basket with these funky pieces of fruit, but don't overload the basket. You want to be able to see all these funky faces looking at you.

- Include a tag on each basket that says it's from the kids at _____ (name of your church or family).

- Once the baskets are complete, it's time to deliver them. You'll want to call an assisted living residence several days prior and tell them what you'd like to do. Try to schedule delivery when everyone is gathered in the dining hall for a meal.

- Two or three kids together will deliver the funky fruit baskets to tables. They will tell the residents about making them and that they'd like to leave them as a gift. Say something like, "We hope this gift makes you smile and brings you joy!" The kids may also want to inform the residents that the fruit is edible after the decorations have been discarded and the fruit has been washed.

- Encourage kids to continue the conversation after they present the fruit baskets. The residents will love talking with the kids!

Discussion

- Read 2 John 1:12 together. Several things about this verse remind us of the

Funky Fruit Baskets project we just did. How do you think this verse applies to what we did?

- How would this project have been different if you had not presented the basket face-to-face?

- Was the project all about the fruit? Is that what the residents needed? Were they short on fruit? *What these people needed most was your attention, your time, your willingness to spend a little time with them, and a reason to smile.*

- What kind of reaction did you get when you presented the Funky Fruit Basket?

- What do you think would be the hardest part about living in an assisted living residence?

- What kind of things do you think these people struggled with when they made the decision to leave their home or apartment and come live here?

- What made you uncomfortable about this project?

- What made you feel good about this project?

- What else could we do for these people?

GRADUAL FOOD COLLECTION

Scripture:

Matthew 25:35 (NIV)

For I was hungry and you gave me something to eat, I was thirsty and you gave me something to drink, I was a stranger and you invited me in.

You Need

- large storage container (box, tub)

What You Are Doing

In this project you will be slowly and methodically collecting food items for donation. Your budget will hardly notice that it's happening.

Who You Are Serving

You are helping supply a food bank or other distribution center that helps those who need food.

Project Instructions

- This project builds weekly as you go to the grocery store, but you must make sure the child goes with you. The child can't just tell you what to buy.

- Each week, give the child one nonperishable food item category. The category could be: pasta, vegetable, soup, fruit, boxed side dish, cereal, sandwich fixings, etc.

- During your shopping, the child must choose one item from that category for purchase along with your groceries. If the category is pasta, he/she may choose a box of spaghetti, a can of ravioli, or a box of Hamburger Helper®. The item just needs to fall within the parameters of the category.

- You will need to designate a box, plastic tub, or shelf at home where the items will be stored.

- As the groceries are put away, add the one item the child chose to the designated container. He/She will watch the storehouse fill. Little ones will want to review the contents of the container every time they add another item.

- When your church, school, or other organization makes a plea for nonperishable food items to donate, your family is ready. Your child can choose which items from your box to take or completely empty your container!

- Take this opportunity for your child to learn about making choices, learn about food groups, and see how a little added on a regular basis can amount to a lot.

Discussion

- What might have happened to cause someone to have no food?

- What did you think about as you chose your item each week? Did you choose things you like?

- How did this ongoing project help us to be prepared for a time when someone needs help?

- What did you learn about putting a little aside each week?

- Read Matthew 25:35 together. "For I was hungry and you gave <u>me</u> something to eat, I was thirsty and you gave <u>me</u> something to drink, I was a stranger and you invited <u>me</u> in." Who is talking here? Who is "me" in this verse? *Jesus.*

- When we feed others, it's just like we're doing that for Jesus. How does that make you feel … to know this food is feeding Jesus?

We're Preparing
to
Give It Away

GROW A GARDEN

Scripture:

Leviticus 23:22 (NLT)

When you harvest the crops of your land, do not harvest the grain along the edges of your fields, and do not pick up what the harvesters drop. Leave it for the poor and the foreigners living among you. I am the Lord your God.

You Need

- gardening tools
- piece of good land
- seeds
- water
- experienced garden planner

What You Are Doing

This takes quite a commitment for several months, but putting out your own garden has enormous benefits.

Who You Are Serving

You will be helping those who don't have money to buy fresh produce, or this could be used as a fundraiser for a different service project.

Project Instructions

- As a family, you could do this project in your backyard. As a church group, we recommend doing this on the church property, if possible. (We'll think of it as a church group project for our instructions here, but don't be limited by that.) You will need an area that is somewhat concealed, can be tilled, is close to a water source, and gets adequate sunlight. You don't want the garden close to the road and visible to passersby who may help themselves. (An experience with stealing is not the lesson we're going for!) If there is not a location at the church, then see if someone in your congregation can provide a garden spot on his/her personal property.

- Recruit someone who has knowledge of setting out a garden to be your overseer.

- As you contemplate what will go in the garden, keep in mind vegetables that can be easily prepared or eaten raw. The people receiving produce may not have access to many kitchen appliances or have cooking skills.

- The Overseer should plan what can go in the garden, the spacing, and the layout. Then show a drawing to the kids who will be participating. Allow time for the kids to ask all of their questions and offer their suggestions. The Overseer should explain why he/she made those choices, but if a suggestion by one of the children makes sense, then by all means incorporate it. This will create huge buy-in for the project from the kids.

- Beforehand, ask someone to come in and till the piece of ground that will be used. So the kids understand how it is done, the tiller should demonstrate tilling the last little piece of the garden while they watch.

- Instruct the children to sit along the edge of the tilled space while you give them instructions on how the seeds or seedlings will be planted. DO NOT put anything in their hands at this point. In their excitement, they will be distracted and will ask a multitude of questions later (that have already been answered).

- The Overseer will demonstrate how each seed/seedling should be planted, not just tell the kids what to do. This is super educational for all the kids and will give them confidence in knowing what to do.

- The kids should be grouped 2 or 3 at a time with a specific instruction for one kind of seed, each group being under the supervision of an adult. The groups will proceed to plant their area/row.

- The kids will water the section(s) they planted according to the Overseer's instructions.

- An adult should be in charge of scheduling kids to tend the garden as it grows. They will be responsible for watering and weeding throughout the season.

- As each type of produce is ready for harvest, distribution must be planned.

If your desire is to give away the produce to those who may not have access to fresh fruits and vegetables:

- Ask the pastor if there is anyone in the church who could use this kind of help. You may want to discreetly deliver a produce bag on a weekly basis to this family as long as the harvest continues. If children are a part of the family that needs assistance, you may want to provide a different way of delivery, other than the children who have grown the garden delivering the produce. This will keep the children who are in need from feeling uncomfortable among their peers.

- Contact a food bank or rescue mission. You will need to make several trips a week (especially if you've planted green beans... they keep on coming!) to deliver the produce. Each time, it is MANDATORY that you take 2 children with you for delivery. They need to experience carrying the boxes/bags and handing them over. They may also get the opportunity to see the people face-to-face who need the produce.

If your desire is to raise money for a different service project:

- Set up an outdoor stand on the property with hours clearly posted. You will need to schedule the kids to work the produce booth. Having it open 3 or 4 times a week, a couple of hours at a time, is sufficient. (People love to pick up groceries on the way home from work.) Keep the hours consistent, so "customers" can count on you being there.

- Outside one of the main entrances to the church, set up a produce stand. Make sure you post prices and what the money raised will go toward. People can purchase their produce as they leave the building after worship.

Discussion

- How did you feel when you planted the seeds?

- How did you feel when you picked your first ripened vegetable?

- What was the most difficult part of this project?

- What part of the project did you enjoy the most?

- How did you feel when you delivered the produce?

- Why did the people we gave our produce to need it? What were their circumstances that they needed help?

- What could change so they would not need our help with food?

- Read Leviticus 23:22 (NLT). How does this verse relate to what we did in our garden? How have we helped the poor with our harvest?

- How do you think God feels about what we did with the harvest of this garden?

- What do you think the fresh produce meant to the people receiving it?

- If we did this next year, what do you think we should do differently?

Because this project takes months and is slow, you will need to provide continual encouragement and enthusiasm for the process. Remind them of what's coming!

HOT CHOCOLATE ON A COLD DAY

Scripture:

Matthew 10:42 (NIV)

And if anyone gives even a cup of cold water to one of these little ones who is my disciple, truly I tell you, that person will certainly not lose their reward.

You Need

- a supply of hot chocolate
- thermoses
- disposable coffee cups
- disposable coffee lids
- napkins

What You Are Doing

The kids will be delivering nice warm cups of hot chocolate in the cold of winter.

Who You Are Serving

The Salvation Army bell ringers stand out in the nastiest weather to ring their bells. Their silver bells remind people to give at Christmas time so that others who have very little will be provided for. A cup of hot chocolate would be a nice treat for these people who selflessly give and never expect someone to serve them.

Project Instructions

- Beforehand, call the Salvation Army and tell them what you would like to do. Ask them for the location of their bells.

- The easiest, and really tastiest, way to make hot chocolate is to heat up some regular chocolate milk you get at the store. (Kroger® brand is incredible for making hot chocolate!) If the brand you purchased isn't quite sweet enough, add some sweetened condensed milk ... oh, yummy!

- Make a big kettle of this warm drink.

- When the cocoa is really hot, fill some thermoses.

- Hop in the car with your thermoses, cups, lids, and napkins. Head to the first Salvation Army kettle on your list.

- Once you arrive and the car is not moving, the kids can fill a cup with hot chocolate (about two-thirds full) and snap on the lid.

- When they hand the cup to the Salvation Army ringer, remind them to thank the person. Say something like, "I want you to have this cup of hot chocolate to thank you for serving God the way you do."

- If you'd really like to go the extra mile, pick up some donuts and deliver one with each cup of hot chocolate!

Discussion

- How often do you think the Salvation Army bell ringers get thanked?

- When you handed the cup to the Salvation Army ringer, what did he/she say?

- Read Matthew 10:42. Does it have to be "cold" water? What is this verse saying?

- Does it take really big things to impress God? *Giving someone just a little drink makes God happy when we do it because we love Him.*

- Is serving God hard? How did this serving experience prove that?

- In what other ways can you give a "cup of cold water" to someone?

Additional Idea for Hot Chocolate

During cold weather, serve cups of warm cocoa to parents as they wait in line at the schools during pick-up time.

KAIROS COOKIES

Scripture:

Hebrews 13:3 (NLT)
Remember those in prison, as if you were there yourself.

You Need

- Ingredients: shortening, brown sugar, granulated sugar, eggs, vanilla, flour, salt, soda, baking powder, chocolate chips
- mixing bowl
- stand mixer
- large cookie sheets
- large pancake spatula
- teaspoons
- quart-size storage bags (without zippers)
- shallow cardboard boxes

What You Are Doing

You will need to connect with your particular state's Kairos prison ministry to see their guidelines. It is very important that you follow these guidelines to the smallest detail.

Who You Are Serving

The kids will be serving prisoners. Kairos is a prison ministry that prisoners opt to be part of. For an entire weekend, they hear the good news of Jesus, build relationships with the men who have gone through training to be with them, hear testimonies from men, and are shown love through special food and gifts. The Kairos missionaries have to remember that the men attending are still prisoners and must adhere to strict rules about what they can bring in and how they conduct themselves. Many lives have been changed through this ministry. One of the ways love is shown to the prisoners is through the gift of homemade cookies.

Project Instructions

- This is a marvelous project for families to do together. Cookies can be made at home and then brought to the point of transportation at the indicated time.

- Contact your state's Kairos ministry for their specific cookie recipe. Each state differs in their guidelines. A group that is planning to present a weekend will have all the information you need. (The recipe we have given you is for the State of Indiana.)

- Follow the instructions on the recipe card for baking the cookies. You MUST use the Kairos recipe. No other recipes will be allowed. Do not change anything! Do not add icing, decorations, nuts, or raisins. Do not use premade, refrigerated cookie dough.

- Package the cookies according to the Kairos instructions. Cool cookies completely before packaging. Don't start packaging them until they are cold. (Chocolate chips take a long time to completely cool.) We suggest putting them on a cookie sheet and quick-freezing them in the freezer before attempting to package.

- Pack them 6 per quart-size bag. These bags cannot have a plastic zipper. Lay them flat in the freezer until ready to pack in a cardboard box, where they need to stay completely flat for transporting.

- Mark the number of bags on the outside of the box.

- Usually Kairos groups will arrange a large truck to transport the cookies. Deliver the cookies at the designated time, so they stay frozen as long as possible. Do not make the cookies at the last minute, or they will not have time to properly cool and freeze.

- Every cookie is inspected before it is allowed in the facility, and any that are oversized, broken from shipment, or stuck together must be removed. That's why you need to follow the directions completely.

Discussion

- Read Hebrews 13:3. How are we living out this verse by making the cookies?

- Why do you think we had to follow the recipe so strictly? *One reason is that the prisoners are so excited to receive for-real homemade cookies that they sit down and eat them all at one sitting. If they were made with really rich ingredients, the cookies would make the inmates sick. They don't get sweet, rich foods much in prison, and when they do, these foods are very limited.*

- Pray over the cookies as they are baking and as you package them. Pray that somehow God will use these sweet little gifts to show these prisoners there are people who care about them because God cares about them. Pray they will confess their bad choices to God and ask for forgiveness. Pray they will receive a brand new life because of Jesus, no matter how long their prison sentence is.

- What is the purpose of the cookies? *It is one way to give the prisoners something special, to make them feel like someone cares about them. You make homemade cookies for people you really care about, not total strangers.*

- Even though you can't go into the prison and see the prisoners who will be eating your cookies, how did this make you feel to contribute in this way?

- What did you learn?

- After the event, invite some of the adults who led the Kairos weekend to share their stories of what happened. This can really point out how important the cookies were, and the kids will get a kick out of hearing some of the reactions. It's not what they would expect! They have no idea how much these cookies mean to those receiving them.

Kairos Cookie Recipe

- 1 c. shortening (not butter or margarine)
- 1 c. brown sugar
- 1 c. granulated sugar
- 2 eggs
- 2 t. vanilla
- 2½ c. flour
- ½ t. salt
- 1 t. baking soda
- 1 t. baking powder
- 2½ c. chocolate chips

Cream shortening and sugar until fluffy. Add eggs one at a time. Sift dry ingredients and add to the creamed mixture. Beat in vanilla. Add chocolate chips and stir by hand. Use a teaspoon to drop dough onto cookie sheets. Bake at 350° until medium to dark brown (13-20 minutes). Cookies should be 2" in diameter.

MATCHING SOCKS

Scripture:

Psalm 133:1 (NLT)
How wonderful and pleasant it is when brothers live together in harmony!

You Need

- a laundry basket of socks
- any socks that do not have matches

What You Are Doing

The kids will be sorting and matching socks.

Who You Are Serving

There always seems to be a basket of socks that never get sorted, matched, and put away. Every time Mom passes them, she thinks, "I need to get to that, but I can't right now." Then, there's the drawer where all the lonely socks go that have lost their mate. Kids will be honoring their parents and voluntarily stepping into family responsibilities by serving in this way.

Project Instructions

- There is no age limit on this project. Even small preschoolers can serve their family in this way. It's developmentally appropriate and good for them too.

- Take the basket of laundered socks to a clear area—bed top or a large table. Try to make it a place where the child will not be easily distracted by TV, conversations, or toys.

- Start laying the socks out in rows. When the next sock you pull out is a match to one that is already down, then put them together. Some families roll the tops down to keep the socks together or completely roll the socks into a ball.

Do this however your family prefers.

- As the socks are matched, put them in piles according to the person they belong to. (This is the part that may be a little more difficult for young kids, especially if they have a teenage brother and father. Whose are whose?)

- Once all the laundered socks are matched, then get out the drawer of socks that have lost their mates. Go through them and see if any matches are among them. If so, put those in the appropriate family member's pile. If there are no matches, return them to the "lost" drawer. Who knows when that missing sock may show up!

- There's one last step. Put the socks away or at least deliver them to the appropriate bedroom if you're not sure what drawer they go in.

Discussion

- Read Psalm 133:1. What does harmony mean? *It means we get along. One of the best ways to get along is by serving one another. When we see a way that we can help a family member and we have the time and skills to do it, then we can invest in family harmony by stepping up to the opportunity.*

- What is "wonderful and pleasant" about harmony?

- How does it make you feel when your family is not in harmony? What can you do about that? *When an apology needs to be made, the apology means even more when both people are able to turn around and serve one another. That says, "It's behind us. We want harmony!"*

- How do you feel when someone in your family helps you out? Does it make you angry? Does it give you a smile? Does it relieve you because it's one less thing you have to take care of?

- The gratification a preschooler gets from being able to contribute to the family in this useful way is tremendous! Don't discount that the foundation for a lifetime servant mindset can be laid at this very young age.

- How long did this project take you? How long will the effects of your act of servanthood last? *A small investment in time can make a difference for a long time.*

MORE THAN A PAIR OF SOCKS

Scripture:

James 2:14-17 (NLT)

What good is it, dear brothers and sisters, if you say you have faith but don't show it by your actions? Can that kind of faith save anyone? Suppose you see a brother or sister who has no food or clothing, and you say, "Good-bye and have a good day; stay warm and eat well"–but then you don't give that person any food or clothing. What good does that do? So you see, faith by itself isn't enough. Unless it produces good deeds, it is dead and useless.

You Need

- new pairs of socks (any kind of adult-sized socks)
- various individually wrapped snack foods
- various small personal hygiene items
- ribbon or shoestring
- copies of the card
- hole punch

What You Are Doing

In this project you will be filling a new pair of warm socks with snack foods and small hygiene items. Once the contents are used or eaten, the recipient is left with a warm pair of new socks.

Who You Are Serving

The full pairs of socks can be kept in your car for those times when you pull up to a stoplight and someone is there begging. These people usually hold a cardboard sign, asking for help. It's difficult to know what to do, because many of these people use the donations they collect to purchase drugs and alcohol instead of food and necessities. On the other hand, if they truly need help, how can you pass by? This project is a small solution to that dilemma.

Project Instructions

- Please do not use old socks for this project.

- In one sock, place small, individually wrapped, snack items (such as: peanuts, pretzels, fruit snacks, sandwich crackers, jerky). Don't include anything (like potato chips) that will crush easily. Fill the sock about two-thirds full.

- In the other sock, place small containers of personal hygiene items—the kind of bottles you get in a hotel room. Good things to include are: toothpaste, shampoo, lotion, mouthwash, and tissues. Again, fill this sock to about two-thirds.

- Run off a copy of the sock note and punch a hole where the black dot is. Fill in the blank with your name (family name or group's name), and cut the sock out.

- Cut a piece of ribbon about 18" long. Run the ribbon through the hole in the sock card.

- Lay the tops of the 2 socks on top of one another. Wrap the ribbon (with sock card threaded on) around the socks, down close to the fill line of the supplies. Tie the ribbon tight and make a bow like you would when tying your shoe. (In fact, you could use a new shoestring instead of ribbon!)

- Now, find a nice clean place in your car to keep 1 or 2 sock sets. The glove compartment or a plastic tub to slide under a seat could be options for your car.

Discussion

- Why is this a good thing to give someone at an intersection, rather than handing that person some money?

- Read James 2:14-17 together. Maybe the person was just trying to get you to give them money to use on some bad choices. But, they also may be really hungry. That isn't for us to decide. We need to be wise in how we handle situations but never decide not to help because we don't know.

- What does James 2:14-17 say to you? What if instead of giving the socks, we just said, "Have a blessed day!

This pair of socks was prepared by the kids at Shorewood Church of God and is a gift for YOU! We thank God that we could offer it to you.

I'll pray for you"? Will that make the person less hungry? How do you think the person would feel toward God and His people if we just said nice words but didn't help?

- How does it make you feel to know you have these socks prepared for the next time you see someone?

- How do you think the person you give these socks to will react? *(Then, once the socks are distributed, talk about what reaction the kids witnessed.)*

Hi!

These socks were prepared by

_____.

I hope you enjoy the goodies in this new pair of warm socks. I want to serve God and help others. If this made you smile, I've done that.

MY OWN BED

Proverbs 3:24 (NASB)

When you lie down, you will not be afraid; When you lie down, your sleep will be sweet.

You Need

- fabric markers
- pillowcases
- pieces of cardboard
- Bibles
- Sweet Sleep video
- games
- Sweet Sleep collection boxes
- mattress
- small pieces of poster board
- regular markers

What You Are Doing

The kids will be having a pajama party and raising money to buy mattresses through Sweet Sleep.

Who You Are Serving

The kids who will be receiving the mattresses are mostly orphans who do not have a bed of their own. They sleep on the ground. An organization called Sweet Sleep provides mattresses and also mosquito nets for children.

Project Instructions

- Purchase a new pillowcase for each child. You can get these online in bulk for $1-$2 each. Wash and dry them, but do not use fabric softener.

- Plan a pajama party for the kids. You can do this with everyone together at the church or have each gender at a separate residence, but basically doing the same kinds of activities.

- The first part of the party will be to raise money. Arrange several work projects the kids can do "for hire" from people in the church. This could be cleaning out brush along a fence line, straightening up a garage, putting down mulch, pulling weeds, scrubbing bricks, or whatever needs to be done that a child could accomplish. Give the kids complete instructions before putting any tools in their hands. The entire "pay/donation" for doing the work will go toward the project.

- Now that the work detail is over, everyone will change into their pajamas.

- It's time to feed those hungry workers. How about pancakes! Pajamas and pancakes go together!

- Show the informational video found on the **sweetsleep.org** website.

- Go through the discussion questions below.

- Provide each child with one new pillowcase and some fabric markers. Slide a piece of cardboard inside the pillowcase. This will keep the markers from bleeding through to the other side of the pillowcase as they work. The kids will open their Bibles to Proverbs 3:24 and write this verse on their pillowcase. They can write it in huge letters across the middle or in smaller lettering across the end opening. Then they will decorate the pillowcase any way they like. Once these are done, lay them out where they can dry thoroughly.

- Play some games, using things associated with sleeping.
  Here are a few ideas:

  - Blindfold one person. That kid will lie on his/her side on the ground with a stuffed animal about one foot in front of his/her chest. The other kids will take turns trying to sneak up and snatch the stuffed animal before the blindfolded kid tags them.

  - See how many people you can cram inside a tent.

  - Get in groups of 3 with each group having a sleeping bag.

The smallest person gets inside the sleeping bag. The other 2 kids in the group will pull him. The groups will race to see who can pull their "sleeping" friend across the finish line first.

- Have a pillow fight.

- Make an obstacle course that includes jumping over a mattress, climbing stairs covered with pillows, rolling across a blanket, and jumping on a trampoline 3 times (like you would jump on a bed), etc.

- Play flashlight Hide and Seek.

- The kids will make an informational display for the church. They can make small posters about what they are raising money for. Then adhere these to a mattress and stand it against a wall where passersby will see. The little posters won't draw much attention on a bulletin board, but put them on a mattress and everyone will take notice! Hang a pillowcase from the mattress with a note that people can contribute by putting their donations in the pillowcase.

- Sweet Sleep makes coin collection boxes available for "Build-A-Bed," and there is no charge for them.

- Set a date and a goal for the money that will be raised. Challenge the kids to find ways they can work for pay. They can also ask for donations, but it's a great character builder if they put forth some physical effort.

- God wants every child to sleep sweetly! It's time to go to bed. Either dismiss the kids to go home to their own beds, or have a place where they will sleep for the night.

Discussion

- Describe your room. Do you share it with a brother or sister, or is it your room all by yourself? What do you sleep on?

- Every once in a while, it's kind of fun to sleep out on the ground under the stars or in a tent. Do you think you'd like it if you had to sleep on the ground all the time?

- Describe the reaction of the children on the video when they received their own mattress. What was your favorite part of the video?

- Read Proverbs 3:24 together. How would the meaning of this verse change if you went from sleeping on the ground to having a soft mattress to sleep on?

How could a mattress help you not "be afraid"?

- Of course, a mattress would be more comfortable than sleeping on the ground, but what other benefits would a mattress provide? *It keeps you up off the damp ground, which would keep the kids from getting sick. Also, it keeps you up away from germs and bugs that are on the ground, which cause sickness.*

- How can we help these kids have a place to sleep? *Set a goal for your group.*

PICK UP STICKS

Scripture:

Philippians 2:4 (NLT)
Don't look out only for your own interests, but take an interest in others, too.

You Need

- absolutely nothing!

What You Are Doing

The kids will be picking up sticks in someone's yard.

Who You Are Serving

When a storm comes through, or just over the natural cycle of seasons, trees lose branches, sticks, and twigs that fall to the ground. These need to be picked up before mowing can begin. For many people, the up and down of bending and picking up is backbreaking work. The kids can surprise someone and offer to pick up the sticks, especially at the end of winter right before the grass starts to grow again. That really would put a smile on someone's face!

The gathered sticks can be used for bonfires, or the person may have a patio fire pit. Before disposing of the sticks, ask if there is a specific place they would like them stacked. Remember, you're trying to make it easier and more convenient for them.

Project Instructions

- Choose someone who lives in a single-family home and has mature trees. This person should be someone who has some physical challenges–who would probably try to do the job themselves but shouldn't because it would be painful. Put some thought into who would get the greatest benefit from having their yard cleared.

- Call the person(s) you have chosen and tell them what you would like to do. Ask, "Would _____ (time and date) be a good time for you?" Don't call and ask them if there's anything you could do in their yard. They will tell you "no." But, if you declare what you'd like to do, what day, and when, then you've given them an easy way to accept your help.

- Before the kids go crazy picking up sticks, instruct them about where the homeowner would like them stacked. Also, show them how they should all go one direction, rather than throwing them onto the top of the pile. This will make it easier if the homeowner wants to use the sticks later. (Think ahead!)

- If larger branches need to be broken down, show the size they should be. Kids love busting up tree branches!

- If the owner would like them taken away or prepared for city pick up, make those arrangements prior to the workday.

- Set the kids loose! More than likely, they will make a competition out of it. Have fun and see how quickly the task can be completed.

- Take a "before" and "after" picture to reinforce the difference they made.

- At any point throughout this project, encourage the kids to talk with the person they are helping. They need the face-to-face time.

Discussion

- How did you feel when you were done?

- Were you tired when you got finished? *Just imagine how the person we were serving would've felt after doing this all by himself.*

- Read Philippians 2:4 together. How does this verse relate to us picking up sticks? Is picking up sticks something kids need to do so they can be better students? *No.* Is it something kids do to get more friends? *No. It's not a normal activity for kids. But, when we look out for the interests of others–for what other people need–like this verse says, then everything we do is not about what we need or want. Our thoughts will be about what other people need! Yeah!*

- I know we made this person happy by taking care of this chore. Did it make you happy to see what you had accomplished and how you had changed someone's day?

- Is this something you would do again? Would you like to do it by yourself or with someone else? Why?

RICE BOWLS

Scripture:

Psalm 82:3 (NIV)

Defend the weak and the fatherless; uphold the cause of the poor and the oppressed.

You Need

- ricebowls from **ricebowls.org**
- hammer
- safety glasses
- rice recipes
- supplies for setting up a church dinner

What You Are Doing

The kids will be collecting money in plastic rice bowls. To raise awareness, they will put together a rice dinner for the church.

Who You Are Serving

This project is to feed orphans in Third World countries.

Project Instructions

- Weeks before you introduce this project, contact **ricebowls.org** to order your FREE collection bowls. You order them 10, 20 or 50 at a time, so estimate what you will need as closely as possible.

- The first thing you want to do when meeting with the kids is to acquaint them with what the Rice Bowls organization is all about. Go to **ricebowls.org** and show two videos. "What is Rice Bowls?" is only 32 seconds long and is an explanation of the project. If you have nonreaders, you will need to read the video to them. The other video you need to watch is "One Fine Tuesday."

It is about 3 minutes in length. Both are wonderful and will get the kids excited about this project. Rice Bowls not only feeds the body of orphaned children but feeds their souls with the hope that comes from knowing Jesus as Savior and Lord.

- Distribute a personal rice bowl to each child. Set a date when these should be returned.

- Each week, read one of the stories from the website about how kids are getting involved and the difference it's making in little lives around the world.

- Divide the kids into groups of 3. They should come up with 5 creative ways to gather funds for their rice bowls. Where would you find money? How could you raise money? Encourage them to figure out how they could work for the money. When asking people to contribute, here's an idea:

  - Carry the bowl with you everywhere. When someone asks what it is, the child will respond, "I'll tell you for a quarter." Once the person deposits the quarter in the rice bowl, the child will explain the project, and then remind the person they could give more.

- Look under the seats in your car and under the couch cushions.

- Together the kids will plan a dinner for the church to raise awareness about world hunger. They will need to plan the menu so that all dishes contain rice. Then invite the church to attend, selling tickets at just the cost to provide the meal. This is not where you are raising funds.

- The kids should research information about orphans and hunger. Videotape them presenting this information and show it the night of the dinner (and maybe on Sunday mornings).

- Present each family with their own rice bowl, along with the date when it will be turned in. Challenge each family to fill their rice bowl with quarters.

- When all rice bowls have been collected, wear safety glasses and smash them with a hammer. Throw the broken bowls in the recycle bin! Then count what you have. This takes some time to sort, roll, and count. It's really helpful if your local bank will sort and count the coins for you in their machine. Take the kids on a field trip to the bank and let them guess what the total will be. Then ... drum roll please ... reveal the amount!

Discussion

- Read Psalm 82:3 together. What does it mean to "defend" the poor and the fatherless? Who are the fatherless? *In Bible times, to be without a father meant you were treated as an orphan. To defend orphans means to stand up for them, provide for them, and fulfill the responsibilities of a parent.*

- What did you learn about hunger and orphans during this project?

- How are the lives of the orphans we learned about different from how you live and get your food?

- How do you think having food changes other parts of these orphans' lives?

- If you heard God's voice talking to you about this project, what do you think He'd say?

- Has anything changed in you from being involved in this project? If so, what?

- How will you pray differently because of this project?

Nearly 163 million children around the world are orphans. This total does not include street orphans, trafficked orphans, or those who are foot soldiers. ("Third Annual Report to Congress..." p 9) Every 4 seconds an orphan dies from malnutrition. ("Goal: Eradicate Extreme Poverty...")

Attention Homeschoolers!

The **ricebowls.org** website has downloadable lesson plans for including Social Studies, Writing, and Math with the Rice Bowls project.

SANDWICHES

Scripture:

Proverbs 22:9 (NLT)
Blessed are those who are generous,
because they feed the poor.

You Need

- lunch meat
- sliced cheese
- bread
- zipper sandwich bags
- condiment packets (mustard, ketchup, mayonnaise)
- forks
- shallow cardboard boxes

What You Are Doing

The kids will be preparing sandwiches.

Who You Are Serving

The sandwiches will be provided to those who are hungry. They can be prepared for a local rescue mission to distribute, or the kids could accompany adults to distribute them to the homeless. You would have to take precautions, but the experience has been successful when thought through. It's a life-changing experience for children who get to participate in it.

Project Instructions

- This is one of those projects that can easily be used with preschoolers, depending on the ingredients you put on the sandwiches.

- Set up an assembly line with the ingredients for making sandwiches. For lunchmeat sandwiches: bread, meat, cheese, bread, ziplock bag, condiment packets. You could also make peanut butter and jelly sandwiches, but don't make them too far ahead of time because the jelly soaks into the bread and it gets mushy.

- The kids should wash their hands thoroughly and wear prep gloves if possible. If not, stick the meat and cheese with a fork as you place them on the sandwich.

- Once the pieces are assembled, slide the sandwich into the ziplock bag. Before zipping it shut, slide whatever condiment packets you have into the bag.

- Lay these flat in shallow cardboard boxes and refrigerate.

- Arrange for delivery immediately following the preparation.

- Make sure the kids are a part of delivering these to the rescue mission or participate in the distribution.

Discussion

- What do you do when you get hungry? Can you usually find something to snack on? What's your favorite snack?

- How is your food situation different from the people we are serving?

- Read Proverbs 22:9 together. What does God want you to know in this verse? *You are blessed ... your life is better ... when you are generous and feed the poor.*

- How is feeding the poor a generous thing to do?

- Where do you think these people get food most of the time?

- What can we do from here?

According to the National Center on Family Homelessness, 1 out of every 30 children in the U.S. is homeless, which is close to 2.5 million kids. ("America's Youngest Outcasts")

SCAVENGER HUNT

Scripture:

Genesis 1:29-30 (NIV)

Then God said, "I give you every seed-bearing plant on the face of the whole earth and every tree that has fruit with seed in it. They will be yours for food. And to all the beasts of the earth and all the birds in the sky and all the creatures that move along the ground–everything that has the breath of life in it–I give every green plant for food." And it was so.

You Need

- copies of the List of Items for Scavenger Hunt
- adult driver for each 3 kids
- tote bags

What You Are Doing

The kids will be gathering food in a fun way.

Who You Are Serving

Once the food has been gathered through the scavenger hunt, donate it to an organization for distribution to those in need of food.

Project Instructions

- Divide the kids into groups of 3 and assign each group an adult driver.

- Give each group a copy of the List of Items for Scavenger Hunt.

- Provide each group with several grocery tote bags.

- Prepare a note of introduction that the kids can present. The note should not tell their names but should indicate what church they are from and what they are doing.

- You can assign each group a subdivision or give them a list of names and addresses of people from the church.

- Give the groups a designated amount of time to "hunt." For each minute they are late returning, one of the items they have collected will not count in their team's tally.

- The groups will go to the assigned neighborhood and, as a group, go to the different homes. You should tell what you are doing and what church you are from. If the people choose to donate, check that item off the list and put the item in the bag. Each household can donate up to 3 items. Express an enthusiastic "THANK YOU!" and move on.

- Return to the starting point by the deadline. Don't be late!

- The kids will want to compare what they were able to collect. Make a tally and see which group was able to collect the most.

- Sort the food items. Put all cans of fruit together in one grocery tote, all vegetables in another, pastas together, and so on. This makes it easier for the place of distribution.

- You have one more trip to make! Load up the totes and deliver them to the organization that will distribute them. Ask if the kids can see where the food is stored and how. Also, arrange for someone to talk to the kids about how the food is distributed.

- If the food is going into the church's food pantry, then the kids should organize it appropriately in that space. Encourage them not to leave the job half done.

Discussion

- What was awkward about the scavenger hunt?

- How did the people react when you told them what you were doing?

- How did you feel about the amount of food you were able to collect in such a short amount of time?

- What do you think may have happened that caused people to need food?

- Read Genesis 1:29-30. God provided all kinds of plants and animals for us to eat. Because of circumstances, some people can't get to that supply God has given. Someone needs to help them get to what God has for them. Who is that? It's the people who have plenty. We don't want to block them from having the food God made for them. We want to be a vehicle that takes it to them.

- What did you learn through this experience?

- How can we continue to help?

List of Items for Scavenger Hunt

_____ can of tuna

_____ can of beef stew

_____ can of chili

_____ can of soup

_____ jar of peanut butter

_____ jar of jelly

_____ can of corn

_____ can of green beans

_____ can of carrots

_____ can of baked beans

_____ can of peas

_____ can of tomato sauce

_____ can of peaches

_____ can of pineapple

_____ can of pears

_____ can of fruit cocktail

_____ jar of applesauce

_____ jar of spaghetti sauce

_____ box of macaroni

_____ box of spaghetti

_____ box/bag of rice

_____ bag of dried beans

_____ box of potatoes

_____ box of cereal

_____ box of crackers

_____ box of graham crackers

_____ bag of chips

_____ package of cookies

_____ package of drink mix

_____ 2-liter of pop

_____ bag of marshmallows

SUPER LONG PAPER CHAIN

Scripture:

Leviticus 19:32 (NIV)
Stand up in the presence of the aged, show respect for the elderly and revere your God. I am the Lord.

You Need

- strips of construction paper
- paper cutter
- staplers
- staples
- Command™ stickers

What You Are Doing

The kids will decorate the hallway of an assisted living facility or nursing home with a long paper chain. This could be done at Christmas but would be even more special if done at a random time of year.

Who You Are Serving

Days are long and lonely when you're ill or just don't have the energy you used to. The kids will be investing in the lives of elderly people in their community.

Project Instructions

- Contact an assisted living facility or nursing home about hanging a super long paper chain down their hallway to freshen things up for the people who live there. They may have requirements about where it can go and about how it can be hung, so make sure you follow these guidelines completely.

- Decide what colors would be appropriate to use at the time of year you'll be hanging the super long paper chain. If it's Christmas, then make the chain red, green, gold, and white. If it's fall, then use orange, yellow, red, and brown. If it's spring, then use pastels.

- Use a paper cutter to make construction paper strips that are 1" wide and 7"-8" long. Don't make them shorter than this, or it will be difficult for the kids to use the stapler. (If it's a Christmas chain, you may want to use ribbon to add a little shine.) You will need several hundred of these to make a super long chain.

- Show the kids the pattern that you'd like the colors to follow.

- Each child will make a chain by first stapling one construction paper strip in a loop. Then they will slide the next color through the original loop and staple it. Continue doing this for your designated time.

- For transporting, it's easiest to keep the chain in individual segments. When you get to the location, then thread one paper strip through the end loops of two sections. Be mindful of the pattern. You may need to add more than one loop to continue with the pattern.

- The kids will spread out down the hallway to hold the chain. They will surely draw some attention from the residents. Encourage them to have enthusiastic conversations with the people they encounter. **It's not the chain that will bring them joy; it's getting to talk with the ones who brought it!**

- Position the Command™ stickers down the hallway, up close to the ceiling.

- An adult will go down the hall to hang the chain over the Command™ stickers.

- Let the kids see you giving out hugs to residents and having conversations. This will help them feel safe and willing to step out themselves.

Discussion

- How did you feel when you went into the facility? Have you ever been inside a place like this?

- What comments and questions did the residents have?

- Read Leviticus 19:32. How were we showing respect for the elderly?

- What do you think the people you talked to will think when they see the chain this week?

- What do you think the people you didn't see or talk to will think when they see the chain this week?

- How was this activity a way of serving others?

- Would you like to go back to visit again? What other things could we do to make their days nicer?

TEA PARTY

Scripture:

Ephesians 4:2 (NIV)

Be completely humble and gentle; be patient, bearing with one another in love.

You Need

- 3-tier serving dishes
- teapots
- teacups
- bite-size snacks
- small plates
- napkins
- assortment of hats

What You Are Doing

In this project the children will be preparing a tea party.

Who You Are Serving

You will be helping a child who is temporarily unable to join in his/her regular activities, due to wheelchair confinement, crutches, or such. The child's normal activity has been interrupted, and he/she can easily feel left out and abandoned by friends. The child gets tired of saying, "I can't do that right now," and this tea party is a wonderful way to bring a little normalcy back into his/her life ... and even make the child feel honored.

Project Instructions

- Make arrangements for a group of friends to have a tea party, and invite a child who is in a temporary recovery situation. Of course, this could also be a tea party that includes a permanently disabled child.

- Three-tiered serving dishes are very important for a proper tea party, but they are also very expensive if you don't have one. An easy, inexpensive way to make one is by getting 2 candlesticks (alike or different) from a dollar store. While you're there, find 3 plates of differing sizes. Wash the dishes thoroughly with soap and water. Completely dry them before starting to "build." Use epoxy glue to attach one candlestick to the middle of the largest plate. Epoxy the other end of the candlestick and set the middle-size plate on it. Now, glue the other candlestick in the middle of this plate, and then attach the smallest plate at the top. Play around with gluing your candlestick upside down, because that usually gives you more plate room. Also, get differing heights of candlesticks. These can be very fun and eclectic ... and the kids can definitely help make them. Wash these dishes by hand and not in the dishwasher.

- The kids will set the table with placemats, small plates, napkins, teacups, and teapots.

- The host children can plan the menu. Encourage them to choose small items that can be eaten with fingers or toothpicks. Include a variety of sweets, vegetables, and appetizers.

  - cherry tomatoes
  - grapes
  - carrot sticks
  - cheese on crackers (use a tiny cookie cutter to cut out the cheese)
  - ham cubes
  - olives
  - small meatballs
  - peanut butter and jelly sandwiches cut into quarters/triangles
  - yogurt covered pretzels
  - hot dog slices with spaghetti (recipe on next page)

- Provide an assortment of hats to be worn during the tea party. Each child can choose the hat they want to wear, but of course, let the Guest of Honor choose first.

- Most kids aren't very fond of tea, but they love chocolate milk or hot chocolate, so serve these drinks from your teapots instead. Little demitasse cups (4 ounces) are perfect for kids and give them an opportunity to pour from the teapot more than once.

- Don't forget to take some photos to send to everyone afterwards!

Discussion

- What "normal" things is your friend missing out on right now?

- How did the tea party help your friend?

- Waiting for your body to heal takes lots of patience. It's nice to have friends who help you pass the time. What else could you do for this friend while they are waiting to be well again?

- Read Ephesians 4:2. How was this tea party an example of "bearing with one another in love"?

- Why was God pleased with your tea party?

Hot Dogs with Spaghetti

These are too much fun! Slice a hot dog into 1" slices. Break some angel hair spaghetti into 4" pieces. Cluster 6-8 pieces of spaghetti tight in your hand and push them through the center of the hot dog slice. You should have equal lengths of spaghetti sticking out both sides of the hot dog. Drop these into boiling water for about 4 minutes and serve.

WELCOME HOME

Scripture:

John 14:27 (NLT)

*I am leaving you with a gift–peace of mind and heart.
And the peace I give is a gift the world cannot give.
So don't be troubled or afraid.*

You Need

- art supplies
- long piece of light-colored bulletin board paper
- one piece of white poster board
- extra-wide marker
- party hats

What You Are Doing

The kids will be forming a welcome home party at the airport for someone who has served in the military. They will be making a banner and a giant card to present to the soldier.

Who You Are Serving

The kids will be serving a soldier(s) who is returning from duty. They will be welcoming that soldier home to a community who appreciates his/her commitment, devotion, and protection.

Project Instructions

- You may have a soldier in your congregation or in a friend's family. Find out the date and time when a soldier will be returning home from duty. Knowing the airline and flight number will also help.

- Before you get the kids together, prepare a long piece of light-colored bulletin board paper. Sketch out with a pencil some giant banner letters that say "WELCOME HOME" followed by the soldier's first name.

- The kids will use markers to decorate the letters. Encourage them to do their best work because that communicates their appreciation.

- Fold a full piece of white poster board in half to make a GIANT card. With an extra-wide marker, write in large letters on the outside of the card: This Card Isn't Big Enough. Then, write on the inside: To Express Our Gratitude.

- Choose one of the kids with good penmanship to write out John 14:27 on the inside cover of the card, towards the bottom.

- The kids will then write their expressions of personal appreciation randomly all over the inside of the card.

- What else could you do to welcome this soldier home? Is there a gift you would like to present him/her? Would you like to put together a basket? Find out if the soldier has a favorite sports team, and then fill a basket with things that identify with the team. How could you add to the welcome home party and personalize it?

- This is definitely a project the kids need to see through to the end. They need to go to the airport to greet the soldier personally. You should be able to get into the baggage return area with your welcoming group. Find out which carousel the luggage will be delivered to and set up your banner.

- Give all the kids party hats. If they think it's silly, just encourage them to think of how overwhelmed they would be if they were the soldier coming home and saw a group of kids celebrating their return.

Discussion

- Read John 14:27 together. Who is talking in this verse? *Jesus is. He's telling us that He has a gift for us. By giving us the gift of peace, Jesus is serving each one of His followers.*

- Why do you think a soldier would be comforted by this verse?

- What is a soldier's main reason for serving? *They want peace and they want the people of our country to be safe.*

- This verse reminds us, though, that even when there's no peace in the world– between countries and different people–God offers us peace of mind and heart. What does that mean? *It means we can lean on God; we can rest in Him. When everything else seems crazy, we can take a deep breath and know that God is with us, and we're okay.*

- How did you serve this soldier today? *We expressed our gratitude that he is willing to put his life in a dangerous situation to protect us. We reminded the soldier that God wants to give him peace of mind, and no one can take that away.*

- How do you think the soldier will remember this day? Do you think this will be a memory he talks about? Do you think he'll tell his soldier buddies? *If he does, then serving this soldier today spread to serving other soldiers.*

IDEAS *for* SERVING

Which Ones Fit You and Your Kids?

IDEAS *to* SERVE YOUR CHURCH

Sanitize

Volunteer to sanitize all the toys in the church nursery. Make sure the kids wear gloves, are given instructions prior to entering the nursery, and have proper supervision.

Ask: "Why is it important for us to keep the toys sanitized? How often does this need to be done?"

Bulk Mailings

Churches don't send out as much U.S. mail as they used to, but special events or campaigns still call for mass mailings sometimes. The kids can volunteer to stuff envelopes, put address labels on, or adhere the stamps.

Roll Silverware

This is something preschoolers can do that helps them feel a part of the church family. For church dinners, the kids can roll the plastic silverware in a napkin. Give those hands a good scrubbing before beginning. Demonstrate and guide the kids on the first few, stressing to get the napkin rolled tightly. Place the finished rolls in the container they will be in on the serving table.

Another option is to make napkin rings by slicing 1" pieces of a cardboard tube with a paper cutter. The kids can glue ribbon around the cardboard tube, then slide the rolled silverware through it. If the tables will be set with silverware prior to guests arriving, then the kids can put the rolled silverware on. Show them how to properly set a table. They can do this!

Spring Spruce Up

There's always lots of sprucing up around the church when spring comes. Include the kids in planting the flowers. (Josh Denhart, a children's pastor from Des Moines, Iowa, shared that his kids trim tons of daylilies on their property and place hundreds of bags of mulch on their 31 islands.) Before putting anything in their hands, though, demonstrate exactly what you want them to do. It may be a little more work for you and take a little extra time, but the benefits are huge. Kids will feel a part of the church family and be reminded of it every time they notice the flowers throughout the summer.

Centerpieces

When having a church dinner, include the children by asking them to make the centerpieces. Pinterest offers many ideas of things the kids could easily assemble to complete the centerpieces. This would also be an optimal time for kids to work with women other than their children's ministry leaders. Partner an adult with 2 kids to put the centerpieces together.

Teach kids how to offer to serve someone.

Before you approach someone, already have in mind what you want to do and when. One of the most UNhelpful things you can say is, "Call me if you need anything." The person won't call! He/she doesn't know what you're willing or able to do. Instead, say, "I'd like to bring you a meal on Monday. What time would be best for you?" People don't like to ask for help, but they will readily accept it if it's offered in the right way.

Rake Leaves

Raking leaves was one of the most fun serving events we ever did. (We lived in Indiana where there are plenty of leaves, and you rake multiple times each fall.) The kids should bring their own rakes. That way, the rake is more likely to fit them. You can also purchase inexpensive child-sized rakes at home improvement stores. Go to an elderly person's home and rake their leaves. Make sure you know what that particular city requires as far as pick up. Some cities want the leaves put in special bags and in others you push the leaves to the street where giant truck vacuums regularly collect them. The kids love seeing the huge piles of leaves they are able to accumulate in such a short amount of time. Take a photo of them in front of their leaf piles, proudly holding their rakes.

Plant Flowers

Be on the lookout for someone who may have a lengthy surgery recovery time, especially during the spring months. Take a tray of petunias to his/her house and ask if you could plant them in the yard. Be aware that there's a commitment to this. Twice a week someone will need to water the flowers, if there's not been a good dowsing rain. You don't want to give the person a gift and then cause him/her more anxiety over how to continue to care for it. When you offer to plant the flowers, assure the recipient that you'll also be caring for them.

Teachers' Helper

It's so frustrating to instruct kids to do something with their markers, only to find out that half the markers are dried up. The kids can go through each classroom's set of markers and toss the ones that no longer function. They can also check the crayons and toss out any little broken pieces. While you're at it, sharpen all the pencils.

Communion Clean Up

On Sundays when communion is served, the kids can be in charge of cleaning up the sanctuary. This means disposing of all the communion cups, and also throwing away bulletins, picking up any garbage, and straightening the standard communication pieces that are kept at the seats. This will make the kids more conscious about what they leave behind each Sunday.

Rewards for Games

Instead of giving novelty prizes or candy for winning games, you can make winning a way the kids can help someone else. You can do this in a couple of ways. At your "prize store," you can have an assortment of canned goods. The winning child will choose which canned good gets donated to the food pantry.

The other way you can do this is to award fake money or points for different things the kids complete or win. One Sunday a month they can take their accumulated wealth and purchase things at the store that will be donated to the appropriate organization. The store could include canned and boxed foods, hygiene items, toys, household items, and clothing accessories.

Puppets

Older kids can prepare puppet scripts and present them to the preschool classes. This is a great opportunity to help the older kids understand that they need to prepare with excellence. It may be "just" a puppet script, but it's done to glorify God, and He deserves our very best.

Sunshine Box

When someone is anticipating a long recovery from a surgery, make him/her a Sunshine Box. Decorate a box in bright yellow paper and write "Sunshine Box" on the outside. The kids will each bring in a small gift for the person. Provide wrapping paper, so the kids can wrap the gift they are contributing. You don't need to indicate whom the gifts are from—just keep it anonymous. If for some reason the packages should be opened in a certain order, then number them. Give the box to the recovering person with instructions to open one gift each day.

Greeters

Adults love to be welcomed to church by a smiling child. Kids represent hope that the church will continue. The kids will be stationed at all the doors of the church. Don't stand there and wait for someone to enter. Be proactive and open the door as people approach. Greet them with a big smile and say, "Welcome to worship!"

Classroom Clean Up

More than likely, you have teaching supplies that need to be returned to the resource center and things that need to be carried to the leader's car. The kids can sign up to be one of the two clean up helpers each week. This will be a relationship-building opportunity for the leader to get to know these two kids, as well as a great relief!

Make Game Boards

You'll need a pencil, some old sheets, and permanent markers. With a pencil, draw a winding trail of large blocks on the sheet to resemble a game board. (Check out games like Chutes and Ladders™ and Candyland™ to see how they are laid out.) There's no right or wrong way—just make sure you have a beginning and an end. The kids can outline the blocks with different colors of permanent markers. Make the outlines wide, so it's easy to tell what color each block is. Give these to classrooms to use for board games ... only they're GIANT and kids can use objects from the classroom as their markers. Assign different responses for each color, such as:

- **RED** – tell a book of the New Testament
- **GREEN** – answer a question about today's Bible story
- **BLUE** – tell a book of the Old Testament
- **YELLOW** – run around the room backwards!

Christmas Eve Service Clean Up

Many churches use individual candles during their Christmas Eve service. There's always a wax mess to clean up afterwards, where candles have dripped onto the sanctuary upholstery. The older kids can help with this tedious clean up task. You will need irons, extension cords, and plenty of paper towels. Before putting anything in the hands of the kids, explain exactly what they should do.

Attach an extension cord to each iron, so you can move more easily around the sanctuary. Make sure the water chamber is empty and turn the iron on its lowest setting. Lay a doubled-over, large piece of paper towel on the place where wax has gotten on the upholstery. Gently rub the warm iron over this paper towel, and you will see the wax coming up through the paper towel. When you see that, move a clean part of the paper towel over the spot. Continue gently rubbing the iron over the paper towel-covered spot until the wax no longer comes through the paper towel.

Make PowerPoint Stories or Announcements

The kids can make outstanding, informational, and memorable stories or announcements using Mr. Potato Heads, action figures, Legos®, or some other toys they have. Recreate a Bible story using one set of these figures. For each scene of the story, set up the figures to depict what is going on. Take a photo of that scene. Give the kids freedom to add scenery and props–oh, the fun they'll have! After you have created and photographed all the scenes of the story, put each photo on a PowerPoint slide. Write a caption to go with each slide. Now the kids can show and tell their PowerPoint story to younger kids.

Kids can also create the same kind of PowerPoint sets to make announcements ... and they don't have to be limited to announcements about children's ministry.

Lead Worship

One of the beauties of the smaller church is that kids can easily be scheduled to participate in leading corporate worship–yes, when everyone is in the same room together! This can be done in a variety of ways and, when incorporated on a weekly basis in some form, changes the way a church views children's ministry. Children come to recognize that worship is not for adults only and that they are part of the church family too. Kids can recite memorized scripture, individually or in a group. If a parent is on the worship team, it's a great opportunity for their child to join them. They can lead motions or sign language to one song, again individually or as a group. Or invite a child to open the service with prayer.

The important thing to convey to the children is that they are serving God. They are NOT performing. They are NOT the center of attention. They are there to help others worship God while they worship Him too, and it should be done with excellence. That means they come prepared because God deserves our very best! These rich experiences have multiple benefits for everyone involved.

Doorknob Detail

Especially during cold and flu season, cleaning doorknobs is a great way to serve the church. Provide kids with sanitizer and paper towels; then go scrub every doorknob in the church. Don't forget that every door has a doorknob on both sides. (You wouldn't believe how many times kids forget the other side!) Dispose of the paper towels often as you clean. Once done, the kids should scrub their own hands as well. You don't want to take home any doorknob residue!

Video Greetings

Kids love to make videos! Why not create an opportunity for fun and serving at the same time. Make available a big assortment of costumes and props. Give the kids a list of people in the church who are recovering from an illness/surgery, who may be lonely, and who need some encouragement. Also, give them a list of people who are celebrating—a wedding, the birth of a child, a new job, or a commitment to Christ.

The kids will create a video greeting card, no more than one minute in length. Challenge them to think about what would be on a greeting card, and then write a short script to say something similar. Use your computer or cell phone to videotape their greetings. These can be delivered in person by taking a laptop on your visit, or they can be shared electronically. No matter how you get the video to the person, it will most definitely make them smile!

Dress-Up Food Drive

Kids have dressing up in mind during the fall months, but fall is also the time when food is needed to distribute during Thanksgiving and Christmas. Challenge the kids to dress up like a food item (a box of macaroni and cheese, a can of peaches, a stalk of celery, etc.) and come to church that way. Use this dress-up activity to promote a food collection the next Sunday. Run your collection by mid-October so the food can be sorted, packaged, and delivered well before the holidays. Ask church staff members to provide you with names of people in the church who may need a food blessing. Make a special card that includes a handwritten prayer to accompany each delivery. Now place the food on the porch, ring the doorbell, and run! No one needs to know who provided the food, because when it comes right down to it, God provided it. He made it possible for you to know there was a need, and He gave you the means to help.

When you serve anonymously, the recipient feels absolutely no obligation to "return the favor" because they don't know who to return it to!

Card-Making Party

Invite someone who makes her own cards by stamping or paper cutting to instruct the kids on how this is done. This will take the kids' artistic abilities and possibilities to a new level and may get them really excited about making a variety of cards.

Along with the kids, create a list of people who would enjoy and be encouraged by receiving a card. Each kid will choose one of those people to make a custom card for, using the technique he/she learned from the instructor.

Bless the Custodian

Surprise the church custodian by decorating the door to his/her workroom. How about cutting out individual giant letters that spell out THANK YOU? The kids can come up with a variety of little gifts they could give the custodian, like a candy bar, hand lotion, or favorite can of pop. Put them all together in a gift bag or basket and include notes that tell the custodian some of their regular responsibilities have been taken care of:

- We've removed the garbage from all the kids' classrooms and replaced the liners.

- We've wiped down and disinfected the countertops in the bathrooms.

- The kitchen floor has been mopped.

Partner with a Cancer Patient

Going through cancer is a long, long process. The patient can get very discouraged and drained of so much energy. If there is someone in your church who is going through cancer, educate the kids on what that means. What kind of cancer is it? What is the person's treatment? How long does it take to know if the treatment is doing any good? What are the side effects of the treatments?

Present the idea of partnering with this cancer patient through his/her entire treatment. Some kids may opt not to be part of this, and that's okay. If only one does, it will be a life-altering experience for that one. Partnering with someone like this means you will stay in touch regularly, offering encouragement and thinking of ways you can brighten his/her day. Commit to how often you will make contact in some way. If you commit to once a week, then you can choose something different to do each day: send a card, call and sing a song you've learned at church, find out what kind of ice cream the person likes and take some over, send a picture of everyone making silly faces, send an e-mail with everyone telling something fun they did that week … let your imaginations go!

Talk to Someone Who Is Alone

Consciously look for people who are standing or sitting by themselves. Talk to people who are alone at a church gathering, or sit in the empty chair at their dinner table. When you talk with them and make the first move, others may be drawn over to talk. Also, look around on Sunday mornings for people who may be visiting or those who just don't seem to have anyone around them. Everyone appreciates a smile, a greeting, and someone to sit with during worship.

Wash Car Windshields

While people are attending an event at the church, the kids can bless them by washing their windshields. Beforehand, instruct the kids in the proper way to do this and to be very conscious of respecting the cars.

Buddy Up

Kids can take turns being a buddy to a special needs child their age or a little younger. Sit down with anyone who expresses an interest in being a buddy and go through what the specific responsibilities are. Through being a buddy, the children will better understand the challenges special needs kids face. We are fearful of things we don't understand, so this helps kids to be at ease in otherwise uncomfortable situations.

Restock the Food Pantry

Kids can get everyone involved in a "Restock the Food Pantry" drive. Explore the book of Amos one week, and talk about how a theme of the prophet Amos was his cry for social justice. The kids will staple a copy of the card below onto a brown lunch bag. (Don't staple the bag closed!) Immediately following church, they will distribute their bags to people other than their parents or parents of kids in their group. Coach the kids on what to say when they offer the bags to people. The card instructs people to place any of the listed items in the bag and return it the following week. Once the bags are returned, the kids will place the collected canned goods in their appropriate place in the church food pantry.

This is a project by the PRESCHOOL class. This morning, we learned about Amos, and his message from God was to help others. We want to help others by stocking our food pantry, so anyone who needs food will be able to eat. You could help us! Place one of the following items in this bag and return it next Sunday to the box by the children's check-in desk.

Thank you so much!

- **Tuna fish**
- **Canned chicken or salmon**
- **Spaghetti O's with meatballs**
- **Spaghetti O's with hotdogs**
- **Canned fruit**
- **Chunky soups with meat**
- **Toothpaste**
- **Shampoo**
- **Conditioner**

IDEAS *to* SERVE YOUR COMMUNITY

DVDs *for Hospital*

Help stock your local hospital's DVD library. Donate G and PG rated movies. As kids outgrow cartoons and other movies from their childhood, show them how giving away something they are no longer using can bring joy to someone else. Include a tag that says, "We pray that God makes your body all well again soon."

Evaluate the service project for age-appropriateness. But, keep in mind, your kids can likely do more than you think they can. Raise the bar and they will meet the challenge!

Undie Sunday

One of the things distribution sites are always short on is new underwear. It's a little awkward to put a package of Cinderella panties or Batman briefs in the collection box. Have a little fun with this, so no one is embarrassed ... we all wear underwear! Declare an Undie Sunday! The kids will lead the way for the church. On a given Sunday, promote that everyone should bring a package of NEW children's underwear to donate.

Backpacks

Right before school starts, school supplies go on sale BIG TIME! Many lower income families do not have the financial resources to equip their kids with all the items they need for their studies. While you're putting together your backpack, buy 2 of everything, and supply a full backpack to a student who needs a good start to the year. Make a bookmark with your favorite Bible verse on it, laminate it, and include it in with the other supplies. These are best distributed by taking them to a school counselor. The counselors know who would benefit from the backpack and can present it with discretion.

Care Baskets for Ronald McDonald House®

When a child is in the hospital for an extended stay, especially when it is in a city away from his/her hometown, parents often stay at Ronald McDonald House® or a similar residence. Snacks out of the vending machine can get costly. Put together a basket for individual families that includes snacks, such as toaster pastries, granola bars, small chip bags, mixed nuts, trail mix, and a few pieces of fresh fruit. (Grapes, bananas, oranges, and apples are all good to include, but just a few.) Include a note to say you understand it's a difficult time, you care for them, and you want to remind them that God cares for them too.

Toy Bucket

Challenge the kids to go through toys they have outgrown, but that are still in tip-top shape, to donate to the children's wing of a hospital. Get a large tub with handles from a discount department store, preferably with a lid. Sanitize the toys that have been collected and place them in the tub. You may want to have 2 or 3 tubs and divide the toys according to age-appropriateness. Attach a tag to the bucket that says, "May God bless you with joy, smiles, and a fun time!"

Make Blankets

The kids can easily make nice, toasty blankets out of inexpensive flannel you purchase at a discount department store. Flannel comes in all kinds of patterns, with sports teams, holidays, children's fantasy patterns, and solids. Leave the material its full width and have it cut at the store to the same measurement as the width. Lay the material out flat and prepare it for the kids by cutting 4" squares out of all 4 corners. Then, make 4" cuts that are ½" wide. Make these cuts all the way around the piece of material (making sure that there are an even number on each side). The kids will take the first 2 pieces of fringe and tie them together in a knot up next to the main part of the blanket. Continue around the entire blanket this way. Deliver the blankets to a homeless shelter or women's/family shelter. Include a tag that reminds the recipient that the blanket is given out of love for God.

Bikes

As kids grow up, they outgrow their bikes. Use these neglected bikes for a great bonding and mentoring activity kids can do with men in the church. Don't pass up this opportunity for kids to have this intergenerational experience. Gather any bicycles no longer in use. (People have these in their garages and storage buildings—what a great time to free up some needed space!) The kids can give the bikes a good cleaning and polishing, and the men can teach the kids how to repair them. Once they are spic-and-span and in great riding condition, add a tag to the handlebar that says, "Enjoy being outside in God's beautiful world! This bike is given to you because we think you're great, and so does God." If you know of a child who could benefit from a bike, take the child who helped fix it with you to present it to him/her. If you don't know of a child to give it to, then contact a family shelter.

Distribute Water

Do you have a large, local athletic event or parade in the middle of the summer? Get permission from the event organizers and fill out any necessary paperwork, so you can give away ice-cold water. Make up labels for the bottles. These should have the name of your group and a greeting, "We are delighted to serve you and our Lord Jesus." Arrange for wagons and coolers. When you get to the location, set the coolers in the wagons. Fill the coolers with bottles of water and then cover completely with ice. If you have the facilities to chill the bottles before loading them for transport, it will speed the process. The kids (accompanied by an adult) will walk through the crowd, offering a bottle of cold water to the spectators.

> ***Consider using the small bottles of water. It gets the same message across, and you can fit more in each cooler.**

Cheerleader

Get a group of kids together and be cheerleaders for the Special Olympics. Give yourselves a special name and have T-shirts made. Get together for a special session before the day of the Olympics, so the kids can write their own cheers and practice them. Get noisemakers and pom-poms if you like. Make this day even more special for the athletes.

Make Placemats

Find out when a Kairos Prison Ministry weekend is taking place and make placemats and handprints for it. These weekends are an opportunity for any prisoners who would like to participate to experience a "spiritual retreat" type of event. The prisoners listen to testimonies, hear the Word of God, and are treated to some special gifts of love. A gift Kairos loves to include is placemats that kids have decorated with verses and pictures. They also like to take cut-out handprints that have messages written on them. The handprints are usually displayed like a wallpaper border. Many times the prisoners will not eat on their placemats because they don't want to get them dirty. They take them back to their cells and use them as artwork for their walls.

Puppies Visitation

Cuddling with puppies or just gazing into their cute little faces brings a smile. Coordinate with a local animal shelter to check out a few of their puppies. You'll also need to make arrangements with a local nursing home or assisted living facility to bring the puppies in. Make sure the puppies are groomed well. Before entering the facility, let the puppies play in the grass a little and "relieve" themselves. Take along anything that may be needed in case of a mishap.

The kids will take turns holding the puppies and sharing them with the residents. This gives an automatic conversation starter. It relaxes the children and breaks down any anxious feelings they may have about talking to an older person they don't know. It also helps them disregard the resident's specific situation. Share the love ... of a puppy!

Teach kids about talking with senior adults and how to ask open-ended questions that start conversations. If the question can be answered with "yes," "no", or in one word, then think about a different way to phrase it. Ask more questions than you answer. Senior adults love to tell their stories, especially if someone young is listening.

Canned Food Collection

Give the kids a unique challenge for collecting cans of food. Determine a set amount of time and try to line cans up against all the baseboards in your room. It takes more cans than you might think! When you've covered the baseboards completely, then just for the fun of it set the kids loose to create something (think building with Legos® and blocks).

Providing food for hungry people helps meet a very basic physical need. Even though we have many programs in our country to help feed children, many kids still go to bed hungry. Think about the potential of each can as it is placed.

Sort Cans

In October and November, local food distribution sites receive a lot of canned goods, which they will distribute during the holidays. In the warehouse where these are stored, much work has to take place in order to get the cans organized. All the beans must be together, all the corn, and so on. Kids—even very young kids—can sort the canned goods. This is a fabulous family activity and a tradition you could participate in every year.

Testimonial

"Our son was 4 and our daughter 2 when we started sorting cans at the local rescue mission. Every year, it was the first activity that prepared our family for the holiday season as they were growing up. Great memories!" –Tim and Val Cuthbert

No More Litter

Choose a park or other public area that needs some attention because of litter. Equip the kids with gloves and large plastic garbage bags. You may also want to give them some kind of tool to help them pick up the gross stuff, because they're going to find it. (They're also pretty fascinated by the pinching tools.) The kids will work in groups of three. That way, one person can hold the bag open while the others make deposits. Ask, "Did you have any idea there was that much garbage here when we began? Can you see the difference we made?"

Grocery Helper

Go to a local grocery store during busy hours. Pair each kid with a teenager or adult. They will station themselves around the parking lot, especially by the handicap parking spaces, and help people put their bags of groceries in the car. Why not pick a day when the weather is not so nice? That would make an even bigger impression on the person you're helping. Remember to return the cart for him/her.

Nursing Home Reading

The kids should bring 1 or 2 children's books with them that they are able to read. Take the kids to a nearby nursing home. The kids will read the books they brought to individual residents. As they read, encourage them to point out things they notice in the pictures. Help kids reverse the roles they are used to playing, so that now they are the adults and the resident at the nursing home is the child being read to. It's fun!

Tray Favors

During holidays throughout the year, the kids can make special tray favors to go with the particular holiday. Deliver these to a nursing home to be included on the trays that are delivered to residents.

Cemetery Flags

Arrange to help put out the individual grave flags at a national cemetery to honor the soldiers who died for our country. Make the call at least a month ahead of time to let the cemetery know of the kids' willingness to volunteer.

Make Cookies

Make some no-bake cookies for community service workers (police officers, firemen, garbage collectors, librarians).

Recipe for Fudge No-Bake Cookies

- 2 c. sugar
- ½ c. cocoa
- ½ c. milk
- ½ c. butter
- 3 c. quick oatmeal
- ½ c. peanut butter
- ½ t. vanilla
- pinch of salt

Combine sugar, cocoa, milk, and butter in a saucepan. Bring this to a rolling boil for 2 minutes. Add the oatmeal, peanut butter, vanilla, and salt. Drop by spoonfuls onto a cookie sheet covered with parchment paper and cool.

Put the cooled cookies in a container and take the kids to personally deliver them. Doing this at a random time of year is even more meaningful than doing it around Christmas. (It would be fun to give the school cafeteria ladies a treat, when they're the ones usually making the treats for the kids.)

If you're doing a group project, make sure every child has a responsibility. Some kids will want to take control and do everything, while others will wait for you to present them with an assignment. Don't take the easy way out and let the outgoing kids do everything.

Bell Ringer

Volunteer to ring the Salvation Army bell. Encourage a parent and child to ring together. This will definitely be a memory-maker. The child will always view the Salvation Army bell ringers in a different light. Ask, "What does the money that is put in the red buckets go toward? How are people helped through this special giving?"

Pack Lunches

The kids will decorate some brown lunch sacks. Prepare sandwiches that do not need to be refrigerated. Include a bag of chips and a packaged cookie. Don't put anything in the bag that may spoil. Take these to a local rescue mission to be distributed. A few or a lot are usually welcome.

Garbage Can Retrieval

A chore no one really likes to do is to bring garbage cans back up to the house on garbage day, especially if the weather is cold or rainy. Gather a vanload of kids who are properly attired and bombard a neighborhood with some good garbage deeds. Grab those empty cans at the street and return them to the house. Make sure the cans are not placed in a location where they will be in the way of a car pulling in or one leaving the garage.

Shuck Corn

Children's pastor Roger Lubiens taught some kids how to shuck sweet corn in preparation for feeding the homeless. What a fun way to teach life skills while learning to appreciate what goes into providing food for someone.

Busy Bags for ER

Children's pastor Cheryl Wilson shared that her kids make Busy Bags for the local hospital ER. While sitting in the waiting room (either as the patient or with someone who is there for treatment), kids need something to do. The Busy Bags provide some activities to keep their attention and help the time to pass more quickly.

Candy Kiss Rosebuds

You'll need stiff floral wire, green floral tape, a hot glue gun, Hershey's Chocolate Kisses®, and red cellophane. The kids will make long-stemmed rosebuds out of Hershey's Chocolate Kisses®. Then, as they stroll through the local hospital, they'll deliver the roses to nurses.

Place a dot of hot glue on the bottom of one candy kiss and then press the bottom of another one into it. They will stick bottom-to-bottom. Cut a piece of red cellophane big enough to cover the candy. Place the point of one candy kiss in the center of the cellophane. Pull the cellophane up and twist it together tightly at the point of the other kiss. Cut a piece of heavy, stiff floral wire 10"-12" long. Lay the twisted part of the cellophane up against the piece of wire. Start wrapping some green floral tape around the cellophane and wire to hold it in place. Continue wrapping the tape until it covers the entire piece of wire. Voilà! You have a long-stemmed edible rosebud and a bunch of happy nurses!

Popcorn

Your church may own a popcorn machine, or you can rent one. Contact a community center in a low-income area. Make arrangements to set up the popcorn machine close to an electrical outlet. You won't have to announce it, because the popcorn fragrance will draw a crowd. Enjoy passing out bags of free popcorn and lots of smiles to the kids who are there.

Welcome Neighbor

Did you spot a moving truck in front of one of the houses on your street? Moving in is hard work! Think of a way you could help. Are there kids in the family? They could sure use a new friend and someone to play with while the furniture goes in and boxes are unpacked. Maybe supplying some cold drinks or some warm cookies would be a way you could welcome them to the neighborhood. If you can't do something on the actual moving day, then prepare a goodie bag to deliver a few days later.

IDEAS *to* SERVE YOUR FAMILY

Serve a Meal

The kids can plan a meal where they show appreciation to their families. Kids are used to parents serving them, but this will be a chance for moms and dads to stay seated while the kids serve them. It gives kids a taste of all it entails to provide a meal.

The first thing each child needs to do is create an invitation that specifies the date, time, and place, and that the child is looking forward to doing this for his/her family. Make the meal something simple, like a potato bar, with a simple no-bake dessert. The kids will do the set-up–tablecloths, handmade placemats, silverware, and a centerpiece. Also, the kids will prepare bowls of potato toppings in the kitchen and put those on the table. With instruction, they can prepare the potatoes and put those in the oven. With a large number of potatoes, increase the baking time (80 minutes at 410°). The children will escort their parent(s) and/or grandparents to their seats. Invite one of the kids to lead the prayer. Then serve the potatoes. Drinks should be filled halfway and put on a rolling cart to take around to the tables. Once parents are finished eating, the kids can serve the desserts. Don't forget about clean up! Moms and dads should not have to lift a finger. Talk about the experience afterwards and see what the kids noticed.

Make a Coupon Book

Provide the kids with printed coupons that make it easy to fill in the blanks with chores they are willing to do. Staple the coupons together. The kids can present a coupon book to their parents with the offer to WILLINGLY provide the service. Think of things your parents would especially like ... good for a foot rub, good for a movie and a snuggle, good for breakfast in bed, good for bathing the dog.

Shoe Scavenger Hunt

Shoes always seem to get scattered throughout the house, and they're never where they should be. Set a timer and see how many shoes you can put away in that amount of time. Make sure you check under the sofa, in the mudroom, behind your chest of drawers, and wherever the dog may have carried them off to. Look what you were able to do in 10 minutes! (And I bet there's one happy mama!)

Alongside Mom and Dad

Very young kids can participate when adults are spontaneously showing compassion. Kids can shovel snow with their little shovels when Dad is helping a neighbor. Kids can rake leaves with their play rakes when a parent is helping a neighbor, or walk alongside with a toy lawn mower when parents are mowing. Kids can add ingredients to a casserole to give to someone recovering from surgery.

Attend a Painting Party

Try to include an elderly member of your family as part of this activity. Many larger cities now have art studios where you take your drink and snacks and make it a social event while you create a painting. The instructor takes you step-by-step through the process, and everyone (no matter how artistically challenged) leaves with a painting they can be proud of. Another option is to invite an instructor to come to you and take kids through the steps of painting a picture.

Some instructors will do home parties to make a Christmas decoration, etc. These are substantial pieces of art/decoration and are quite nice (no matter the age of the person doing them—even preschoolers can be guided through). Many times these people will come for free for the opportunity to get exposure for their business, since it's such a niche industry. Once the painting is done, visit the elderly relative you had in mind and surprise him/her with this piece of art!

Label the Day

Sometimes we just need a reminder to get something done. It's way too easy for the week to slip by, and we do not get around to something we really intended to do. Taking care of your area of the house is a way to serve your family. A kid's room always seems to need some attention. A little picking up each day will help you find the bed, but a bedroom needs a major overhaul about once a week. There's always something better to do, though. So label ONE day of the week with one of these names—10-minute Tuesday, 6-minute Saturday, 15-minute Friday, 13-minute Thursday. Choose which one you'll commit to.

Set a timer for the number of minutes that go with your label. While the timer is on, there will be no distractions. This is a full-force, go-all-out, take-the-mountain attack! See how much you can get done in that amount of time, and when the timer goes off, you're done.

Make it a competition with siblings. Take a photo of each room BEFORE the timer, and then another photo AFTER the timer buzzes. Who made the biggest difference in his/her room?

> Verbally acknowledge when a child spontaneously helps someone. The best praise is done in private. Rather than saying, "Good boy," "Great job," or doing something that calls attention to the act of service, discreetly say, "I saw what you just did, and that was awesome. I'm sure God was pleased." You don't want the praise to become the motivator.

Make a Serving Jar

Fill a jar with rolled up slips of paper. Each slip will have one small task a family member can do for someone in the family. Some ideas to put on the slips are included here, and don't hesitate to add or duplicate the ideas. The child decides if he/she is going to pull out a slip every day, once a week, specific days of the week, etc. After the jar is assembled, put it in a noticeable place where seeing it will be a reminder. On the days the child has decided on (and this should be a voluntary decision and commitment), he/she will draw out one slip first thing in the morning. Once the task has been completed, then put the slip in a different jar. This way, when all the slips have been pulled from the original jar, a new start-over jar is all ready.

- Compliment each person in your family.

- Pray for each person in your family.

- Clear everyone's dishes after a meal.

- Make someone's bed.

- Give 5 surprise hugs.

- Sort some laundry and put away another person's clothes as well as your own.

- Read to a younger sibling.

- Empty the bathroom trashcans.

- Draw a picture for someone.

- Write a note to a grandparent.

- Write a thank you note to someone in your family.

- Play a game with a sibling and let them choose the game.

- Dust the living room furniture.

- Leave a surprise for someone.

Video Chat with a Grandparent

Many children live far away from their grandparents. As much as the kids miss out on having a grandparent around, the grandparents miss out on day-to-day growing up events. Believe it or not, video chatting is a way to serve your grandparent. The child will pick out a favorite book and get on Skype or one of the other video chat programs. The child will read the book to the grandparent, stopping to put the pictures up to the screen … making it just like they were sitting together on the couch. You've made a grandparent very happy!

Invite a Family

As a family, serve another family. Choose a single mom or dad (and their kids) that you may not know very well. Invite them to join you for lunch after church or for a picnic. To really serve them, make sure your family takes care of all the details, and it's just an enjoyable time for the guest family.

IDEAS to SERVE YOUR WORLD

Cards to Soldiers

Make cards to send to soldiers. Encourage kids to get really creative with the cards they make. Soldiers enjoy letters and hearing about what kids are doing, so include a letter inside each card. Make sure everything you say is positive and uplifting. Tell a story of something funny that happened to you! You will want to glue or staple this on the inside of the card because you don't want the letter and card to get separated. The cards should not be put in individual envelopes. The kids can use markers or colored pencils, but DO NOT use stickers, glitter, or confetti. Put all the cards in a large manila envelope and send them to: A Million Thanks, 17853 Santiago Blvd. #107-355, Villa Park, CA 92861. They will see that soldiers receive them.

Operation Christmas Child

Kids love to participate in collecting shoeboxes for Operation Christmas Child. Show one of the videos on **samaritanspurse.org** to the kids. This will help them realize the need for the shoeboxes and the eternal impact they make.

For an added impact, paint the shoeboxes brown several days in advance. Give the kids sheets of nativity stickers to place on the outside of the boxes. Then the kids will make a card for each box to remind the recipient of the birth of Christ.

Gather all kinds of items that can be put in the shoeboxes, along with items that should not be included. Play a simple game of "yes" and "no." When you hold up an item, the kids will have to tell if it's something that can go in the shoebox or not. The kids will lie on the floor. If the item can go in the shoebox, they will kick their feet in the air. If it shouldn't go in the box, then they will stay still. Some of the items that should not be put in the boxes are: candy that melts (chocolate), toy guns or anything military related, lotions, aerosol cans (no silly string), medications, anything breakable, or used items. Things that can be included are: school supplies, jewelry, socks, hats, non-liquid hygiene items (toothpaste, toothbrush, comb), hair clips, small toys...AND...a picture of you!

Think ahead! If you know this is a project you are going to do annually, then collect items at different times of the year. July and August are good months to collect school supplies because they're on sale then. Declare one month "dental hygiene" month and another "stuffed animal" month. How about a toy month and a doll month! When it's time to pack the shoeboxes, you'll already have a good supply of things to put in them. You'll be surprised at how many more boxes you'll be able to pack.

Because they already have everything they want or need, some children make their birthday party into a shoebox party, where everyone brings items to fill shoeboxes instead of gifts for the birthday kid. Set a goal for your kids and see how they can creatively gather shoeboxes. Information on where to deliver the boxes is on the Samaritan's Purse website.

Collect Eyeglasses

People in many countries do not have insurance or the money to pay for glasses. The glasses we no longer think are stylish or ones that are not our prescription any longer can be reused for someone with a similar prescription. Make up an e-mail template that explains you are collecting used glasses and wondered if the person would have a pair to donate. Then state when the glasses will be collected. In the e-mail, ask the person to respond, so you know whom to visit for collection. Children will ask their parent(s) to send this e-mail out to people on their e-mail contact list. Arrange a time when kids can go with a sponsoring adult to pick up the glasses. The glasses can be sent to the Lion's Club. Optometrists who go on mission trips connect with the Lion's Club for eyeglasses to distribute. They act as a storehouse for glasses that are needed by all kinds of organizations.

Family Mission Trip

Kids can go on mission trips! We're not used to thinking this way, but more and more families are being encouraged to do mission trips together. One of the organizations that encourages families to come together is Back2Back Ministries, which focuses on orphan care. You can view a video about what happens in a typical day on one of these trips by going to **back2back.org**. Unlike many mission trips where the visiting group completes a construction project, Back2Back has everyone with the orphans all day long. Visitors eat with the kids, help them with homework, play with them (especially soccer), and just get to know the orphans. It would be a great way for a family to spend a vacation!

Fill an Action Pack

Go to the Voice of the Martyrs website at **persecution.com**. Preview the information and decide what you will show the children. We are blessed in the United States to be able to worship without fear, but that is not so in many other parts of the world. By exploring this website, the children will learn about the risks Christians in other countries take by sharing their faith in Jesus Christ.

Order 1-4 Action Packs. This is a way that Voice of the Martyrs encourages Christians around the world. Each bag costs $7.00, which is the cost of shipping it overseas. With the bag you receive a list of suggested items to place inside. The kids will bring one of the items to contribute to the Action Pack. Encourage them to do an extra chore to get paid, so they can purchase the item themselves, rather than asking a parent to buy it. When the Action Packs are distributed, Voice of the Martyrs adds a Bible or Gospel storybook.

Gather the kids around the Action Packs, asking each child to place one hand on a pack. Pray fervently over these packs and the situations our Christian brothers and sisters find themselves in.

Pack Dental Kits

When churches sponsor mission trips, they try to take things they can leave behind. Many people take an extra suitcase of clothes, and once they wear them, they give them away. One of the things people in Third World countries cannot afford is good dental care. The kids can put together dental kits that can be distributed by the people going on the mission trip. Contact toothpaste companies and ask for donations. Dentists will often give toothbrushes or dental floss. Each kit (small plastic bag) should contain: toothpaste, toothbrush, and dental floss. Including a small mirror would also be nice so the person can see his/her fresh new smile.

Ask the people delivering the dental kits to take a picture, so the kids who put them together can see the faces of people who were served by their generosity and work.

Buy Livestock

Through Compassion International, you can provide livestock to a family in a Third World country. Watch the 2-minute video (**compassion.com/livestock**) about how the gift of livestock can change a child's life. The children in the recipient family love caring for the animals, which provide milk, meat, transportation, and more. They learn excellent life skills and help their families.

Decide what you would like to purchase as a group: chickens, pig, cow, donkey, goat, sheep. Then come up with a plan for how you will raise the money. Is there something you could give up—a birthday present, money for snacks at the ballpark, or something you could put in a yard sale—in order to raise the money?

> *Colton, a 2nd grader, was told he could put only 2 things on his Christmas wish list. The list came back with only one thing written on it—a pig. A pig? Why did Colton want a pig? In his class on servanthood, he learned about the impact one pig could have on a family, and his heart was touched.*

Emergency Response

Kids hear the current news reports, and they are concerned about those who have been affected by floods, tornadoes, tsunamis, fires, and other disasters. The need in these instances is usually immediate and requires a spur-of-the-moment response. Help kids connect with these emergency situations and avoid a helpless feeling. Contact the Red Cross, the Salvation Army, and your denomination headquarters to be put on a list to be contacted when there is a need like this.

Work out a plan with your kids of what they would like to provide. They may want to collect supplies to make emergency bags that have toiletries in them ... or they could collect new stuffed animals for kids who have lost everything ... or they could collect baby clothes. Work on getting your supply together, so the kids can respond immediately when notified.

SIX-WEEK

Servanthood

PROGRAM

Before You Begin

Before you begin this intensive 6-week program designed to help your kids open their eyes to the needs around them, here are some things you'll want to consider:

Read through all 6 lessons before beginning. This will give you an idea of plans you need to make or supplies to gather before the week of the lesson. You will also see how the 6 weeks fit together.

Gather information. Weeks before the *Unwrapping the Servant* program begins, you will need to request brochures and catalogs from service organizations for the first session. Recruit some people to help you brainstorm information you could provide the kids.

Get permission slips signed. Rather than deal with this each time you go off-site for a service project, get a permission slip signed at the very beginning to cover all the activities.

Emphasize that this program requires a 6-week commitment. If kids will need to miss a week, then ask them to consider coming the next time the program is offered so they can participate in all 6 weeks. The objective of this program is life-change, and the main way this happens is through focused study and experience. Missing out on a week will greatly diminish the outcome. Stick to this rule, even if your group is very small in size. Once others hear about the incredible things the kids did, they will be more ready to invest in the commitment the next time.

Allot the amount of time you will need for your meetings. The first 2 weeks will require about 90 minutes per session. On weeks 3-6 you will need about 2½ hours. This will allow you plenty of time for the lesson, travel to your location, the project, and debriefing.

The leader has 2 responsibilities.

1. Make it happen! The leader's responsibility is to take the kids' desires into consideration and complete the planning in areas where they are not equipped to make the decisions.

2. Another important responsibility is to talk constantly about how the group is serving God. People get an impression of what God is like by the way we serve them. You will drive kids deeper in their faith by helping them understand they don't have to wait until they're older to put their faith in action. They are not the church of tomorrow. They are the church of today!

Sample Invitation

Send a special invitation to the kids to promote the 6-week program. Below is a sample, but please feel free to create your own.

Hey kids, this is Pastor Tina!

When you unwrap a present, you find a special surprise inside.

I want to invite you to get **"UNWRAPPED"** and find out what's inside YOU that God wants to use **RIGHT NOW!**

Each Saturday for 6 weeks, starting Oct. 9, I want to spend time with a very special group of 2nd & 3rd graders (10:30-12:00).

God calls all of us—even kids—to serve Him by being His hands and feet in our world. Let's **UNWRAP** the talents you have for serving Him.

Hope YOU will be able to join me!

WEEK 1

Listen to Music Together

Download "If We Are the Body" by Casting Crowns. Pull up the lyrics on your computer and project them so the kids can see the words. Listen to this song together and talk about the chorus.

- Who is the body? Who is the "we" referred to in this song? *As believers and followers of Christ, we are His body. While Jesus prepares a place for us in heaven, we're supposed to continue on with the kinds of things He did when He walked this earth.*

- What are we supposed to be doing as the body of Christ? *We are supposed to reach, heal, teach, help, and go to people–not wait for them to come to us– and love them.*

- What keeps us from doing those things? *Fear of what other people will think. Feeling superior to someone in a bad situation. Being comfortable with the people we're friends with. Not wanting to spend the time because we're already busy. Not seeing that people really need help. What other reasons?*

Open Individual Boxes

In preparation a week or two before the program begins, contact parents for a photo of their child. Then, for each child who has signed up for the program, write an individual note. This note should communicate the potential you see in that particular child and share your excitement for what you are beginning together. Express that you are convinced God will unwrap something in that child that will change his/her life. These notes should be handwritten and unique for each child. This is very important! (See a sample letter on p 132.)

On a sticky note write: "In 6 weeks you will probably look the same as this photo, but something inside you will be totally different." Stick this note to the back of the photo.

Place both the photo and the individual note you've written in a small box (not an envelope) and wrap it. Mark the outside of the box with a gift tag, indicating which child it is for. Give all the children their boxes at the same time and instruct them to find a quiet, private place to open their gift.

Complete the Pretest

Make copies of the pretest we have provided for you, which consists of 10 multiple-choice questions. Prior to passing out the pretests, give all instructions. The kids are to choose only one answer for each question. Emphasize that there are NO wrong answers, and they will get an A+ if their answers are completely truthful. That's all you're looking for—truthful answers.

Give each child a pretest and a pencil. Seat the kids so they're not close to one another. Make sure they write their name on the paper and give it to you. That's the last they will see of their test.

Videotape a Discussion

Set up a video camera and record a discussion you lead with the kids. Do not try to video this yourself but have someone else take care of that. (This is a wonderful opportunity to bring another adult, who is not involved in children's ministry, into the session in a nonthreatening way.)

Encourage the kids to talk honestly and openly. Present each of these questions and encourage as many kids as possible to respond.

- What do you think of when you hear the word "serve"?

- What do you think Jesus had in mind when He told us we were to be servants?

- What kind of opportunities have you had to serve?

Save this videotape to show at the last session.

Open Your Bibles

Read together Acts 2:43-47 (NLT): *A deep sense of awe came over them all, and the apostles performed many miraculous signs and wonders. And all the believers met together in one place and shared everything they had. They sold their property and possessions and shared the money with those in need. They worshiped together at the Temple each day, met in homes for the Lord's Supper, and shared their meals with great joy and generosity–all the while praising God and enjoying the goodwill of all the people. And each day the Lord added to their fellowship those who were being saved.*

- How did the believers in these verses serve one another?

- What did they do together?

Read together John 13:12-17 (NLT): *After washing their feet, he put on his robe again and sat down and asked, "Do you understand what I was doing? You call me 'Teacher' and 'Lord,' and you are right, because that's what I am. And since I, your Lord and Teacher, have washed your feet, you ought to wash each other's feet. I have given you an example to follow. Do as I have done to you. I tell you the truth, slaves are not greater than their master. Nor is the messenger more important than the one who sends the message. Now that you know these things, God will bless you for doing them."*

- This passage happened at the last meal Jesus shared with His disciples. It was one of the last things He taught them. Why do you think Jesus washed the feet of His disciples?

- What does this passage say about thinking you are better than someone else?

- What should we be willing to do for others?

- When Jesus washed the disciples' feet, it was a symbol of the lifestyle we should have. We are not meant to do a good deed every once in a while but to find ways to serve all the time.

- It wasn't Jesus' job to wash their feet, but He did. Have you ever not done something because someone else was supposed to take care of it? We should always be willing to step in and serve someone else.

Serving Wall

On a large wall, post 4 signs that will designate 4 areas of service: Family, Church, Community, World.

Say: *"In the next 6 weeks, we're going to concentrate on serving in these 4 areas. There are other ways we could divide our serving opportunities, but these are the ones we'll concentrate on."*

Give markers and a supply of yellow cards to the kids. To make the cards, simply quarter sheets of yellow card stock. On each card, the kids will write a way they can serve someone in one of the 4 areas. If it's a way they can serve their family, then they should adhere the card under the "Family" heading on the wall. Don't help them in any way with clues. These ideas should be purely what they think of on their own.

Talk About It

What is the single craziest thing God has ever asked you to do?

God is calling us to do something CRAZY in these 6 weeks. He wants us to affect this place where we live–our homes, our church, our town, and our world. How do you think we'll be able to do that?

Homework

Make a copy of the homework sheet (found on p 136) for each child. Throughout the week, the kids are to notice 10 places where someone needed help–big or small. They should write each one on a separate line and make sure they are all different.

The kids do not have to do anything about the situation. The need could even be one they see on a TV show or cartoon. The object is to get them to notice there are lots of needs around them. You will discover many of the kids will end up with more than 10 because they've started opening their eyes!

Sample Letter for Gift Boxes

Dear Millie,

I am so excited about what will happen in the next 6 weeks! I don't know what God is planning, but I know you and I are going to be changed by this experience. It means so much to me that you wanted to spend this time with me, doing what God wants us to do.

When I think of you, Millie, I see a sweet girl who loves her friends and family. I see someone who is quick to do something, rather than sit back and watch. Just last week, when Eric was having trouble holding the pieces of his craft together, I saw how you left what you were doing to help him. God loves that kind of spirit.

I believe you'll discover some things about yourself and about the world we live in during **unwrapping the Servant** that will help you serve our God in bigger and better ways.

Let's see what He has for us.... Here we go!

Pretest

Name: _____

1. Being around people who are poor:

   _____ frightens me

   _____ makes me sad

   _____ makes me want to help

   _____ doesn't bother me

2. How old should you be to volunteer to help in your town?

   _____ at least 18

   _____ at least 15

   _____ at least 12

   _____ other age - _____

3. Being a "servant" means:

   _____ doing what I can whenever I can

   _____ working for someone else

   _____ doing whatever I'm told to do

   _____ doing yucky stuff

4. I notice places (outside of my own home) where I could help:

_____ every day

_____ once in a while

_____ never

_____ only when they are pointed out to me

5. In order to help someone, there must be:

_____ an adult in the group

_____ at least 3 people

_____ one willing person

6. The reason I offer to help someone is:

_____ they will pay me

_____ they need help and I can do it

_____ they've done something for me before

_____ my parents tell me to

7. When someone is sick, most of the time I:

_____ pray for them

_____ stay away from them

_____ try to take them something special

_____ try not to think about it

_____ talk to them about their sickness

8. How many times can you think of that you served someone this week?

_____ 0

_____ 1 time

_____ 2 times

_____ 5 times

_____ 10 times

_____ other _____

9. I can think of _____ ways I could serve today.

10. Name one thing you want to learn while you're involved in *Unwrapping the Servant*.

"Unwrapping the Servant" Homework

Your mission this week is to identify 10 times when you see someone who needs help. You do not need to do anything about it ... just write it down.

1. _____

2. _____

3. _____

4. _____

5. _____

6. _____

7. _____

8. _____

9. _____

10. _____

WEEK 2

Review Homework

The kids should have brought their homework sheet with them, identifying 10 times during the week when they saw someone in need of help. Many of them will probably have more than 10 listed on their papers.

Give the children an opportunity to share with the group what they wrote down. Rather than have one child read all of his/her responses, take turns letting each child share one. Do as many rounds of this as you have time for.

Explore Resources

You will need to gather information from various organizations that provide assistance. The greater your variety of information, the better. You could also provide Internet access (preferably on a device with a decent-sized screen) for groups of 2 or 3 kids to browse the corresponding sites. Both printed copies and websites have their advantages for this activity. Many organizations have videos online the kids can view. Some national/international organizations who offer catalogs and brochures are listed here, but there are many more. Make sure the organizations you choose to introduce are serving in the name of Christ, though, and are not just community, humanitarian, good-deed types of organizations.

- Children of Promise (echildrenofpromise.org)

- Rice Bowls (ricebowls.org)

- Compassion International (compassion.com)

- Sweet Sleep (sweetsleep.org)

- Back2Back Ministries (back2back.org)

- Operation Christmas Child (samaritanspurse.org)

- Hands and Feet Project from Audio Adrenalin (handsandfeetproject.org)

- Voice of the Martyrs (persecution.com)

- World Vision (worldvision.org)

- Feed My Starving Children (fmsc.org)

- Feed the Children (feedthechildren.org)

- The Water Project (thewaterproject.org)

Also, gather local information from your community organizations, such as food pantries, rescue missions, home-building projects, etc.—anything that is specific to your area.

Now provide the kids with colored cardstock cards (other than yellow from last week) and a permanent marker. The kids will work in groups of 2 or 3 to explore the information you have gathered. As they come across an idea of how they could serve, one person will write that idea on one card. Each idea goes on a separate card. They can make as many cards as they want. The objective is to help them see there are plenty of people who need help and endless ways kids can actually be the ones who provide that help.

The kids should not limit themselves to only what they find in these catalogs and websites. During this session, they can include any ways they think of to serve others. Many of the resources provided here focus on the international scene, but encourage the kids to think about family, church, and community also.

You will be blown away by the intensity with which the kids approach this activity!

Play a Game

From last week, you should have 4 categories identified on the wall: Family, Church, Community, and World. The yellow cards from the beginning of this intensive 6 weeks should still be posted to represent the ideas the kids had about serving.

Keep the kids in the same groups they were in when they reviewed the catalogs and websites. To play this game, each group will need a similar-sized bucket and some beanbags. (Ball pit balls work also but take more time to retrieve.)

Determine a stand behind line for the kids to toss from. Don't make this difficult—you want them to be successful often.

One person from each group will begin tossing beanbags at the bucket. As soon as he/she gets 3 beanbags in, he/she will take one of the cards created in the last activity and tape it under the most appropriate heading. The next person in the group will immediately start tossing to get 3 beanbags in the bucket. (The more beanbags you have available for the game, the more fun it is and the faster the game goes. You can get more cards on the wall that way.)

Post any leftover cards under the appropriate heading(s).

Discussion

Let's talk about servanthood. Being a servant is not just about doing good deeds. Servanthood is a lifestyle—a way you think—and not just something you do every once in a while.

Look up the following verses and talk about each one before moving on to the next:

- **1 Timothy 6:18 (NLT):** *Tell them to use their money to do good. They should be rich in good works and generous to those in need, always being ready to share with others.*

- **Hebrews 13:16 (NLT):** *And don't forget to do good and to share with those in need. These are the sacrifices that please God.*

- **James 4:17 (NLT):** *Remember, it is sin to know what you ought to do and then not do it.*

- **James 2:14-16 (NLT):** *What good is it, dear brothers and sisters, if you say you have faith but don't show it by your actions? Can that kind of faith save anyone? Suppose you see a brother or sister who has no food or clothing, and you say, "Good-bye and have a good day; stay warm and eat well"—but then you don't give that person any food or clothing. What good does that do?*

Activity

Isn't it amazing how many ideas we came up with—our wall looks so different now. I'm sure some of these ideas make you think, "That's not me. That's not anything that interests me." But I also bet some ideas on the wall get you excited, and you're thinking, "I hope we can do that one!"

Give each of the kids 2 small stickers. They will choose 2 of the cards on the wall, under any headings, that interest them most. They should adhere their stickers to those 2 cards.

Prayer

Put each of the headings on slips of paper and put them in a container. Draw one out. All the children will assemble under that portion of the wall. Today, pray specifically for the people who fall under this heading, whether you know them or not. Pray that God will give them hope and that this group will be able to show God's love through serving them.

What's Next?

Discuss the projects that have the stickers on them but also bring the other cards into this discussion. Over the next 4 weeks, the group will be doing 4 projects—one in each area: family, church, community, and world. Work together to decide which project you will take on under each heading.

Lead the children in brainstorming what they will need to do to prepare for each project.

- What equipment and supplies do we need?
- Will we need extra adult supervision?
- Will we need transportation?
- Who will contact the organizations?
- On which week will we do each one?

Choose which project will be part of your meeting time next week. As the leader of the group, your responsibility is to make the arrangements that will make each project possible. The kids will be able to do some minor things, but you will need to take care of things like calling a facility to get permission to come and work there or scheduling the church van. If the kids have planned the serving activities for all 4 weeks, then it will be much more time-efficient for the leader to make plans for everything at the same time.

WEEKS 3, 4, AND 5

Weeks 3, 4, and 5 are set up the same. The main activity of the week is carrying out the service project the kids chose to do the week before.

Add to the Wall

Always give the kids a chance to add more ideas to their serving wall under the appropriate headings. As they learn about and experience serving, they naturally will see more opportunities. The big objective for this course is to open their eyes to the needs around them. The idea wall is visible evidence of that.

Show a Video

Each week, show one of these videos or another similar one you've located. Create a serious atmosphere by turning down the lights and lowering your voice as you introduce it. The kids will watch intently and have lots of questions.

- Samaritan's Purse has multiple videos of varying lengths to share what happens when you contribute an Operation Christmas Child shoebox (**samaritanspurse.org**). You can even track where your box goes.

- Watch a Water Purification video (**csdw.org**) that shows how one small packet can clean 10 liters of nasty water in just 30 minutes. The organization will also send you a sample packet if you like. This site is produced by Proctor & Gamble and is not done in the name of Christ, but it has great visual aids for educating your kids on any water-related project.

- As you watch a video from Sweet Sleep (**sweetsleep.org**), your kids will be moved by the fact that some children do not have a bed to sleep on. As the video ends, you see a huge number of children walking down a path, balancing their new beds on their heads.

After the kids have viewed the video, talk about what they saw. You probably will not have to ask many questions. They will have plenty of their own as a reaction.

- How are these children like you?

- How are they different from you?

- How did watching this video make you feel?

- What did this video make you want to do?

- Is this problem too big for us to try to help?

- What happens when someone reaches out, sacrifices, and helps in this situation?

Listen to a Song

Music is powerful, and many songs have been written that point toward serving. The lyrics to each song can be found on the Internet. Project the words for the children, so they can easily follow along and be able to review what the song says.

For each of these 3 lessons, download one of these songs and listen to it together:

- **"Kings and Queens" by Audio Adrenalin.** The video is also really fun to watch. The band celebrates and plays with the orphans in Haiti, where they sponsor communities and families. Other videos explain why the band wanted to write and record this song.

- **"The Generous Mr. Lovewell" by Mercy Me.** *What is the main message to you in this song? How could you be like Mr. Lovewell?*

- **"Give Me Your Eyes" by Brandon Heath.** Watch the YouTube video. This song is a prayer. He is talking to the Lord about how he usually acts, what he noticed, and then asks God to give him eyes to see what people around him are going through. *What happens at the very end of the video? He starts letting people know he cares.*

Prayer

Before beginning work on your project of the week, share a time of prayer together. Help the kids understand all the facets of the project they can pray about. (This will be caught more than taught as the kids hear you pray.)

Pray that:

- They will make a little difference in someone's life today.

- They will do a good job.

- They can have a good conversation with someone they are serving.

- They will be safe.

- God will change their lives through this experience.

- People will understand this act was done because we follow Christ.

Complete Your Service Project

Make sure you leave plenty of time to complete whatever project the kids chose to do this week. If they need to bring a special piece of equipment (like a rake), send out an e-mail reminder the day prior to your regular meeting time. You should have secured permission slips at the beginning of the course, and you will need to have them with you if you go off-site. Also, plenty of adult supervision is needed, especially when going off-site.

Once the work on the project is completed, do not neglect to have a time of debriefing. This is critical for changing the mindset of the children.

- How did this experience make you feel?

- Were we able to help? How?

- What went really well?

- What could we have done to make this a better experience for everyone?

- Will this person ever need help again? Why?

- What caused this person/group to need help? (Were they sick, poor, lonely, addicted to drugs?) What is the root of the problem?

- Is there something that needs to happen for this problem to go away?

Next Week

Before dismissing, you will need to make sure everyone knows what project the group will be completing next week. Are there any responsibilities the kids need to take care of in preparation?

WEEK 6

This is Celebration Week!

Complete Posttest

As you did the very first week, give the kids a test–the posttest (found on p 148). This is exactly the same multiple-choice test as the pretest, except for question 10. They should go off by themselves and answer the questions with all honesty. There are no right or wrong answers. As you compare the answers from the pretest with these answers, you will likely see drastic changes.

After they have turned in their posttests, have the kids spend some time talking about how they feel they have changed. You may want to point out how you've seen individual kids change.

Show Video

Show the video you made during Session 1, where the kids discuss what they think serving means.

- How have you changed since we made this video 6 weeks ago?
- Would you give the same answers?

Project

This is a great week for the kids to invite a significant adult to join them. It's the perfect time to choose a project (maybe something for the church) that will require some strength adults can provide. (This was always the week we cleaned out the church barn!)

During the course, the kids should have completed one project for each area: **family, church, community,** and **world**.

Celebrate

Put together a PowerPoint photo album of the kids' participation in activities over the last 5 weeks. They will enjoy seeing themselves and sharing this with the adult they brought with them.

Provide some kind of party. Go to a fast food restaurant together, have a cake, throw water balloons at one another...! The Bible is full of times when people celebrated because they had completed the assignment God gave them. Let's not forget to celebrate!

Prayer

The kids who have participated should join hands in a circle. The adult they invited should stand behind them with hands on the child's shoulders. Thank God for the experiences of *Unwrapping the Servant* and for stretching you, and ask God to keep your eyes open to needs that are opportunities to serve Him.

Posttest

Name: _____

1. **Being around people who are poor:**

_____ frightens me

_____ makes me sad

_____ makes me want to help

_____ doesn't bother me

2. **How old should you be to volunteer to help in your town?**

_____ at least 18

_____ at least 15

_____ at least 12

_____ other age - _____

3. **Being a "servant" means:**

_____ doing what I can whenever I can

_____ working for someone else

_____ doing whatever I'm told to do

_____ doing yucky stuff

4. I notice places (outside of my own home) where I could help:

_____ every day

_____ once in a while

_____ never

_____ only when they are pointed out to me

5. In order to help someone, there must be:

_____ an adult in the group

_____ at least 3 people

_____ one willing person

6. The reason I offer to help someone is:

_____ they will pay me

_____ they need help and I can do it

_____ they've done something for me before

_____ my parents tell me to

7. When someone is sick, most of the time I:

_____ pray for them

_____ stay away from them

_____ try to take them something special

_____ try not to think about it

_____ talk to them about their sickness

8. How many times can you think of that you served someone this week?

_____ 0

_____ 1 time

_____ 2 times

_____ 5 times

_____ 10 times

_____ other _____

9. I can think of _____ ways I could serve today.

10. Name one thing you learned while you were involved in *Unwrapping the Servant*.

INDEX *Scriptures for 25 Service Project Plans*

(In Biblical Order)

- **Matthew 19:21 (NIV) (Family Scavenger Hunt, p 46)**
  Jesus answered, "If you want to be perfect, go, sell your possessions and give to the poor, and you will have treasure in heaven. Then come, follow me."

- **Matthew 25:35 (NIV) (Gradual Food Collection, p 54)**
  For I was hungry and you gave me something to eat, I was thirsty and you gave me something to drink, I was a stranger and you invited me in.

- **Luke 10:34 (NIV) (Boo-Boo Basket, p 21)**
  He went to him and bandaged his wounds, pouring on oil and wine. Then he put the man on his own donkey, brought him to an inn and took care of him.

- **Luke 24:46 (NLT) (E-mail a Missionary, p 43)**
  And he said, "Yes, it was written long ago that the Messiah would suffer and die and rise from the dead on the third day. It was also written that this message would be proclaimed in the authority of his name to all the nations, beginning in Jerusalem: 'There is forgiveness of sins for all who repent.'"

- **John 4:13-14 (NLT) (Clean Water, p 33)**
  Jesus replied, "Anyone who drinks this water will soon become thirsty again. But those who drink the water I give will never be thirsty again. It becomes a fresh, bubbling spring within them, giving them eternal life."

- **John 14:27 (NLT) (Welcome Home, p 92)**
  I am leaving you with a gift–peace of mind and heart. And the peace I give is a gift the world cannot give. So don't be troubled or afraid.

- **Ephesians 4:2 (NIV) (Tea Party, p 89)**
  Be completely humble and gentle; be patient, bearing with one another in love.

- **Philippians 1:3 (NLT) (Care Packages, p 24)**
  Every time I think of you, I give thanks to my God.

- **Philippians 2:4 (NLT) (Pick Up Sticks, p 75)**
  Don't look out only for your own interests, but take an interest in others, too.

- **Hebrews 13:3 (NLT) (Kairos Cookies, p 62)**
  Remember those in prison, as if you were there yourself.

- **James 2:14-17 (NLT) (More Than a Pair of Socks, p 68)**
  What good is it, dear brothers and sisters, if you say you have faith but don't show it by your actions? Can that kind of faith save anyone? Suppose you see a brother or sister who has no food or clothing, and you say, "Good-bye and have a good day; stay warm and eat well"–but then you don't give that person any food or clothing. What good does that do? So you see, faith by itself isn't enough. Unless it produces good deeds, it is dead and useless.

- **1 Peter 3:8 (NIV) (Compassion Center, p 37)**
  Finally, all of you, be like-minded, be sympathetic, love one another, be compassionate and humble.

- **2 John 1:12 (ESV) (Funky Fruit Baskets, p 51)**
  Though I have much to write to you, I would rather not use paper and ink. Instead I hope to come to you and talk face to face, so that our joy may be complete.

WORKS CITED

"Goal: Eradicate Extreme Poverty and Hunger." UNICEF -. Web. 11 May 2015.

"New Sesame Street Muppet Helps Children Learn Life-saving Hygiene Habits." World Vision. 7 Jan. 2015. Web. 7 May 2015.

"The Second International Conference on Nutrition: Committing to a Future Free of Malnutrition." Food and Agriculture Organization of the United Nations, 19 Nov. 2014. Web. 7 May 2015.

"The State of Food Insecurity in the World (SOFI) 2014." Food and Agriculture Organization of the United Nations, 23 Sept. 2014. Web. 7 May 2015.

"Third Annual Report to Congress on Public Law 109-95, the Assistance for Orphans and Other Vulnerable Children in Developing Countries Act of 2005." 1 Dec. 2009. Web. 11 May 2015.

"#WaterEffect | Just Add Water. Change a Life. | World Vision." World Vision. 23 Jan. 2015. Web. 7 May 2015.

"Willow Creek Association | MOVE - What 1,000 Churches Reveal About Spiritual Growth." Web. 11 May 2015.

NOTES

NOTES

NOTES

CPSIA information can be obtained at www.ICGtesting.com
Printed in the USA
LVOW05s0839270515

439961LV00003B/5/P